Believe-in-You Money

Believe-in-You Money

What Would It Look Like if the Economy Loved Black People?

Jessica Norwood

Berrett–Koehler Publishers, Inc.

Berrett-Koehler Publishers, Inc.
1333 Broadway, Suite 1000
Oakland, CA 94612-1921
Tel: (510) 817-2277
Fax: (510) 817-2278
www.bkconnection.com

ORDERING INFORMATION

Quantity sales. Special discounts are available on quantity purchases by corporations, associations, and others. For details, contact the "Special Sales Department" at the Berrett-Koehler address above.

Individual sales. Berrett-Koehler publications are available through most bookstores. They can also be ordered directly from Berrett-Koehler: Tel: (800) 929-2929; Fax: (802) 864-7626; www .bkconnection.com.

Orders for college textbook / course adoption use. Please contact Berrett-Koehler: Tel: (800) 929-2929; Fax: (802) 864-7626.

Distributed to the U.S. trade and internationally by Penguin Random House Publisher Services.

Berrett-Koehler and the BK logo are registered trademarks of Berrett-Koehler Publishers, Inc.

Printed in Canada

Berrett-Koehler books are printed on long-lasting acid-free paper. When it is available, we choose paper that has been manufactured by environmentally responsible processes. These may include using trees grown in sustainable forests, incorporating recycled paper, minimizing chlorine in bleaching, or recycling the energy produced at the paper mill.

Library of Congress Cataloging-in-Publication Data

Names: Norwood, Jessica, author.
Title: Believe-in-you money : what would it look like if the economy loved Black people? / Jessica Norwood.
Description: First edition. | Oakland, CA : Berrett-Koehler Publishers, Inc., [2023] | Includes bibliographical references and index.
Identifiers: LCCN 2023010698 (print) | LCCN 2023010699 (ebook) | ISBN 9781523004638 (paperback) | ISBN 9781523004645 (pdf) | ISBN 9781523004652 (epub) | ISBN 9781523004669 (audio)
Subjects: LCSH: United States—Economic conditions | United States—Race relations. | Businesspeople, Black—United States—Economic conditions. | Businesspeople, Black—United States—Social conditions. | African American businesspeople—Economic condtions. | African American businesspeople—Social condtions.
Classification: LCC HG4910 .N67 2023 (print) | LCC HG4910 (ebook) | DDC 338.6/4208996073—dc23/eng/20230512
LC record available at https://lccn.loc.gov/2023010698
LC ebook record available at https://lccn.loc.gov/2023010699

First Edition

31 30 29 28 27 26 25 24 23   10 9 8 7 6 5 4 3 2 1

Book production: Westchester Publishing Services
Cover design: Tigist Kelkay

*For Black founders—especially my parents—
who dream and build worlds where
our joy and our imagination can thrive.
Thank you.*

Contents

Preface

What would it look like if the economy loved Black people?

When I look at our economy today, one thing I see clearly is a lack of love for Black people. The reality of the racial wealth gap makes this truth undeniable: a Black person has the least amount of wealth in the United States—just one-eighth of the average White person's wealth.[1] This relative lack of wealth comes from generations of financial exclusion and racial terror, and it affects everything from quality of education and health care to access to wealthy networks, political power, and, of course, business capital. Because of pervasive and ongoing systemic racism, Black founders are denied business loans twice as often as any other group and receive less than 1 percent in venture capital.[2]

Yet, the myth of the American Dream has indoctrinated us to believe that entrepreneurship and capitalism will save the day, that they will somehow close the wealth gap for Black people and provide a pathway for stability and well-being in Black communities. But let's be honest. The only way that a system based on racism and extraction can ever do these things is by engaging an explicitly antiracist and community-centered approach.

Believe-in-You Money delves into the history of Black business investing and shares six profound ways we can all use capital as a powerful tool for addressing racial injustice. By offering practical guidance and story-based evidence, the book invites all people—wealth holders and wealth movers—to start a money revolution that realizes the power of investing in Black business owners and culture makers in a way that creates a better tomorrow.

By reimagining risk and providing nonextractive, long-term, antiracist capital to Black founders, we can make transformational and long-lasting changes. When our practices and policies truly honor and invest in the brilliance and innovation of Black people, we will all reap the collective benefits of a more just, equitable, interconnected, and loving society.

Introduction

No More Bootstraps

Watching my parents as business owners was one of the most influential experiences of my early years. I especially looked up to my mom, who got her start as a young woman in the tech field, specializing in education software design. Later in life, she expanded her entrepreneurship, becoming a published cookbook author and comanaging the Black Boaters Summit, a travel company for Black people who love sailing. She also traveled the world with her husband, Paul. She made a stunning life for herself that was full of adventures and left an indelible impression on me.

What my parents' example helped me realize is that business owners can create the world they want, rather than simply accepting or recreating the world that's been handed to them. My mother was a powerful example of what some folks now call Black world making, and watching her in action was liberating for me. Back in 1992, when she launched her education technology company, lots of people were getting rich in the tech world, and Mom hoped to be one of them. Instead, the White guys were given the green light for success. Today, when I read data from a Project Diane report that says Black women in technology get less than 1 percent of the billions of dollars in investment capital, it's clear that Mom never stood a chance at getting the capital she needed to get her dream off the ground.[1]

It wasn't until Mom's death that I realized that her beautiful, rich, entrepreneurial life was supported by bootstrapping. Bootstrapping is often framed as a positive, praiseworthy thing; finding a way to survive despite having no outside financing is an impressive feat, right? In reality, a bootstrap beginning is the best indicator that a company will have cash problems that ultimately slow growth. What I call Believe-in-You Money is my proposed way to interrupt the widespread need for bootstrapping among Black business owners.

Right now . . .

The median wealth of White families is $141,900 and only $11,000 for Black families.[2]

How we got here . . .

Given that our current economic system evolved from the history of chattel slavery in the United States, which treated African people as commodities, the vast inequities between White and Black families are unsurprising. In the time since chattel slavery was outlawed, Black Americans have been overrepresented in the underpaid service industry and often excluded from careers that support accumulation of money and generation of wealth.

Which means that . . .

Black entrepreneurs have more barriers to successfully launching their businesses. Given the glaring racial disparity in median wealth, combined with the overall segregation of our country, Black business owners are less likely to have people in their personal networks who can provide capital to finance their early business growth. While Black people have disproportionate access to wealth, we do not have any fewer excellent business ideas, which means that this gap in capital results in good businesses being unable to secure funds to get their ideas off the ground.

The narrative of bootstrapping as an impressive feat has gone unquestioned for far too long, with far too little attention on the inequities embedded in the feasibility of the practice. A long history of discriminatory policies created wealth inequality that makes bootstrapping an unevenly helpful endeavor. For example, Black veterans were denied access to the GI Bill, a post–World War II piece of legislation that offered benefits such as housing, a college education, and vocational classes. The practice of redlining, which strategically uses neighborhood limits to discriminate against people seeking financial and other rights, has disadvantaged Black people in several ways, including compromising their ability to secure fair mortgages and other types of loans. And further, the structural relationships that created the racial wealth gap make bootstrapping impossible for most people of color. Emphasizing the importance of bootstrapping—instead of transforming the unjust systems we've continued to embrace—makes Black Americans' struggle to accumulate wealth about personal responsibility and failure rather than acknowledging the role that extractive capital in business financing plays in disadvantaging Black business owners.

The collective American belief in bootstrapping is a hallmark of capitalism and evokes images of rugged individualism and the iconic so-called self-made man. American society is so devoted to the myth of bootstrapping that it ignores the evidence that this false narrative is hurting many of us, particularly Black business owners and other entrepreneurs of color. Bootstrapping tells us to be dependent on no one and nothing but ourselves. It tries to make us believe that a little bit of hard work and sacrifice can make anyone a millionaire. But in reality, we're almost never doing anything alone, and people who become millionaires often receive far more financial support than those who do not become millionaires. Coming from a safe and loving home, having people around you who value education, and having friends and family with significant cash to spare are all factors that make success much more attainable. Perhaps the worst thing about the bootstrap myth is that it makes us think that working ourselves to the bone is the only way to be valued or appreciated.

To change these circumstances . . .

We must transform our practices, attitudes, and beliefs around how we support and invest in Black-owned companies.

Because . . .

Despite the current overrepresentation of Black women launching businesses, less than 1 percent of venture capital goes to Black-owned companies (which means that only a fraction of 1 percent is going to Black woman-owned companies). Black women have an estimated need for $15 billion per year in investment capital. And when it comes to loan capital, Black-owned companies are turned down by the bank three times as often as other entrepreneurs.

As a result . . .

Owing to weaker pre-pandemic bank relationships and funding gaps, over 41 percent of Black-owned businesses closed during the COVID pandemic as opposed to just 17 percent of White-owned businesses.[3]

What we need now . . .

We need a revolution for investing in Black-owned companies. We need the Believe-in-You Money approach, a set of guiding principles that create the type of investment that taps into abundance, redefines the things that really matter, and trusts the recipient. We need a revolution in our capital placement that repairs historical damages, values diverse contributions, honors Black culture and other non-White/non-Western cultures, and commits not just to personal wealth growth but also to seeing our broader communities thrive, collectively.

Right now, this type of investing in Black companies is obstructed by systemic racism and implicit biases that continue to create barriers for Black entrepreneurs' success, ultimately widening the wealth gap. There has to be a better way to provide capital to Black founders. When do we ask for more? After seeing business after business close during the pandemic—the most recent evidence of this hundreds-of-years-old crisis—I am convinced that now is the time to come together and move away from transactional, extractive relationships and into transformational ones rooted in trust and belief in a better future.

We need a revolution in which we transform our existing investment infrastructure into one that institutionalizes an experience of abundance rather than scarcity. After all, how can we invite abundance into our lives if the system continues to insist that there's not enough for all of us?

This revolution requires something important: belief. Belief is powerful because it is the first step toward having a vision and then making a plan of action. We have to believe that change is possible and that we can move away from an extractive capital model and into one that encourages us to believe in one another and to embody our belief through just and equitable practices and policies that put us in right relationship with one another. By unlocking our sense of imagination and possibility, we can invest in Black-owned businesses and work together toward a future that feels good for everyone.

Believe-in-You Money is all about the abundance that comes from seeing resources beyond a scarcity framework. Instead of looking at what we don't have, we must take note of what—and, most importantly, *who*—we do have. Black communities have brilliant people who could be and ought to be solving the world's most pressing problems. It's time we invest in them.

This book is for all the people who love Black-owned companies—investors (like me), business owners, folks in philanthropy or banking, and social justice warriors that care about ending systemic racism. For all of us who see that something more powerful can be done, if we agree to make the change.

I'm inviting people to start small. Start where you are. You are the investor. If we can just power that part of ourselves, we may be able to reach a whole other level. We'll stop thinking that the power to make this change happen is somewhere outside of us. The power is *in* us, and it requires us to simply shift what we believe is possible. If you believe that this is possible, that we have what we need, then all it takes is for us to actually open those doors and those pathways to one another. But it has to start with believing it's actually possible, and noticing that it is you and me who can make it happen.

My Mother's Legacy

My mother had a beautiful office in downtown Chicago on Michigan Avenue and a growing list of impressive clients. But none of that mattered in the financial world. She wasn't going to get the capital, support, or visibility she needed to succeed, simply because she wasn't a part of the favored demographic. Seeing my mom unable to access the capital she needed planted the seed for what became my life's work. RUNWAY, the financial innovation firm I founded in 2017, is where I carry out my commitment to transform investing practices and provide Black companies with the kind of capital people like my mom need—the kind of money that demonstrates belief in Black founders and commitment to their success.

Two weeks after RUNWAY's soft launch, Mom called me with devastating news—a call no one ever wants to get. She had pancreatic cancer. I immediately put everything related to RUNWAY on hold for the following year. I didn't know if the momentum I had been building for the company would still be there in a year's time, but I knew that I had to spend that time with my mom.

I made the right decision, as my mom died 11 months later. The night she died, I was cuddled up with her on the sofa. She laid in my arms as if I were the safest place in the world. She had been moved to hospice care and was barely eating or sleeping; but in my arms, she rested deeply. My mom was like so many of us; she started her business because she wanted freedom and flexibility that she couldn't get by working for someone else. But the problem is that Black founders are just as likely to encounter the glass ceiling on their entrepreneurship journey as they are inside an office. Most of the founders I talk to want a relationship with capital providers who have the background, understanding, and willingness to relate to them. And they don't tend to want a public exit or to grow to some unrecognizable size. They're in business because they love what they do, they want to effect change, and they want to build generational wealth.

On her final day, Mom asked me to get her purse. She pulled out a note she had written. "What's this?" I asked. A list of names and amounts of money were written in her handwriting. She responded with clear instructions, saying, "Go into my bank account and refund my customers." It was still important to her to take care of her business. She then looked at me and said, "Jess, there is so much I want to tell you." I imagined it was about who needed to be paid back, but she said, "I want you to know that love is all that matters. It is the most important thing in the world and we take it for granted sometimes, but it's all that truly matters."

Mom's last words shifted me deeply. Why did she use her last breaths to tell me about love? Was love that important? Her words pulled me into a universe of possibilities where love was at the center of everything. How my mom cared for her customers, that was love, too. Soon, a question began to settle in my heart, and it became my North Star: What would it look like if the economy loved Black people? *Believe-in-You Money* is my answer.

Love, Repair, and Money

Believe-in-You Money is about bringing love, repair, and money together. It's about how we enter into love, how we work intentionally to repair racial injustice, and how we use the resource of money to transform things around us for the better. Believe-in-You Money is the beloved community in action, using money to repair the impacts of racial bias that Black founders face.

Believe-in-You Money is about belief—belief in something you have never seen. This idea starts with the needs of Black founders, but truthfully, it is a way of thinking about deploying reparative resources that can be used everywhere and benefit everyone. Rooted in Afro-Indigenous practices that guide us in sharing resources responsibly and cooperatively, Believe-in-You Money was designed especially for women, creatives, culture makers, start-ups, and anyone who has ever been financially marginalized.

This book is for you, the beloved community investor. I call you an investor because if you are reading this, you are investing in a future that is calling on a new economic reality—one that releases racial bias and sees and honors the contributions of all people. If you have ever wanted a Black business owner to succeed, regardless of how much money you have, then you are in the Believe-in-You Money club. Together, the investors in our community connect because they want to see a change in how we invest in Black companies. And if we work together on this, using a shared framework, we can transform the capital experience for Black founders, particularly at the start-up phase.

This book is about an idea whose time has arrived. There are calls for more humane capital from every corner of the world. These calls are coming from women founders, culture makers, workers, and visionaries who know that, if they could just get the money they need to operate fully, they could create powerful positive outcomes for themselves and their communities.

I believe in a future that includes Believe-in-You Money for all. Even though it has never happened, I know it is possible. I don't need to know the future to believe in it. Bound and chained, our ancestors couldn't see that this day would come, a day when their daughter is publishing a book for all the world to read, talking about a new financial moment that brings love, repair, and money together, with an explicit emphasis on repairing the wrongs done to people of the African diaspora. But here I am! I come from people who worked hard, had tremendous faith, and never needed visible, tangible proof to believe that a better world was possible.

This book is inspired by big and beautiful ideas about how to change things, now, from where we are. As you read, you will get an insider's perspective about investing in right relationship to Black founders. Each chapter contains my thoughts alongside a conversation with someone whose work is committed to building an economy that loves Black people. Some folks are artists and activists, some are spiritual healers and teachers, and others are investors and entrepreneurs. They all carry a powerful thread that's weaving an economy that loves us all.

Much of what I've learned from these wisdom keepers—from our conversations in this book and from witnessing them in their work over the years—has come to guide my investing strategy. Thanks to this community, I look for the places that can be healed, and I find ways to use money as a salve for the wounds of the past. Believe-in-You Money is one of the most powerful tools for doing so.

Chapters 1 through 3 share stories that provide background on how I came to this work and what I learned along the way, as well as background on what Believe-in-You Money is all about and who is moving this kind of capital. Chapters 4 through 9 take each of the six foundational characteristics of Believe-in-You Money and unpack them through story, historical context, and conversations with wisdom keepers, investors, and culture shapers who are actively moving investments to Black founders in a powerful way. The final chapter wraps it all up with a call to action, at which point you get to decide how you'll **join the Believe-in-You Money revolution!**

What This Book *Isn't*

This is not a how-to book. Because every investor is different and their motivations, capacities, and approaches vary, I did not want to be prescriptive about how someone should use the information in this book. For people moving money, I have found that this book is best viewed as guidance—not a playbook—that offers six foundational characteristics to consider when investing in Black founders. For people who are not moving money but care about investing for racial equity, this book can be a great teaching tool. Knowledge is power, and so the more we all know about community-centered capital as an alternative to conventional investment capital, the more we can bring this type of money to the forefront.

Also, this book is neither exhaustive nor fixed. The ideas in this book are a start, a foundation. But this book alone does not define the wholeness of what is possible when working graciously with Black founders and creators. I imagine that, as we collectively evolve our experience toward investing in right relationship, we will decide that other things matter to our analysis. This book offers six ideas that I see as crucial, but again, the possibilities are certainly not limited to just the ones I share in the book.

Finally, and importantly, this book does not present an alternative for capitalism. I struggled with how much I wanted to share about capitalism, because as long as capitalism requires inequality, Black and Brown people will always be economically excluded. That's because capitalism works in tandem with racism.[4] In order to close the wealth gap, we have to use regenerative wealth strategies, which are in opposition to capitalism, even as we continue to exist within a capitalist economy. It feels sticky to avoid the reinforcement of capitalist trauma when working with business and money. It's truly a dilemma. This book acknowledges this dilemma, and instead of talking about what *is*, I use this book as a tool to encourage readers to think about what *could be* if we take the approach of Believe-in-You Money.

I know that we aren't there yet.

Closing the racial wealth gap will require multiple interventions from private and public actors. *Believe-in-You Money* joins a chorus of ideas in the solidarity economy landscape that prioritize people over profits. From municipal bonds to baby bonds and everything in between, there are many ideas that are intended to catalyze wealth for Black people and to simultaneously challenge capitalism as they gain traction. Part of the motivation for this book is to activate our imaginations and think about what it looks like to show love to people instead of leveraging financial power to effectively punish the people with less capital by caring more about profit than our fellow humans. How can we create an evolved economy if we do not include a vision that loves Black mothers, workers, and business owners?

The concepts presented in this book are most often found in postcapitalism conversations, which tend to call for a return to Afro-Indigenous ways of organizing community, sharing responsibility, and sharing resources. By bringing these concepts to Black business spaces, I hope to offer a pathway to our collective transition into the next economy—an economy that loves Black people.

What This Book *Is*

Believe-in-You Money is a guide for anyone who wants to center authentic relationships and prioritize power building and wealth building as they move capital to Black founders.

This approach can be used at any stage of investing in Black companies, but Believe-in-You Money is most powerful at the very beginning of the business journey. Offering Believe-in-You Money early on in a capital journey equips founders with more flexibility and a better position to access information, seek clarity, and build relationships that will help grow their business. Instead of the founder depleting their personal savings only to navigate without sufficient guidance, we can illuminate their path with business education, transparent conversations, and a shared understanding of investor expectations and needs early on. When we move from this place, power grows.

Power Building

What do I mean by power, and why is it so important? The financing system overwhelmingly focuses investments in Black-owned businesses narrowly, investing only in immediate, short-term success. This model allows only a small number of Black and Brown founders to get ahead and ignores the masses of Black business owners with transformational business ideas that they're unable to launch simply because of their socioeconomic status. We will catalyze the long-term systems change that Black founders need only by reshaping our approach. Building power is about supporting the people and communities that are most affected by structural inequities—the founders, the workers, the residents that patronize the business—and helping them develop, sustain, and grow an organized base that can act together. The website of the Praxis Project articulates that community power relies on "democratic structures to set agendas, shift public discourse, influence who makes decisions, and cultivate ongoing relationships of mutual accountability with decision makers that change systems and advance equity."[5] Power building addresses the root cause of inequities: disenfranchisement.

Dr. Martin Luther King Jr. said that "power properly understood is nothing but the ability to achieve purpose. It is the strength required to bring about social, political, and economic change."[6] We know that the interests of those with systemic power—folks who have money, institutional knowledge, or control of the resources—are the most prominent in our political, social, and economic environment. Focusing our investments on people, ideas, and funds corrects the power imbalance between money holders and founders and positions the people affected and harmed by racial inequality to set the agenda and drive the self-determined outcomes that they seek.

Advancing Women

Believe-in-You Money helps advance Black woman entrepreneurs and any other founders struggling to navigate a financial maze that is both unclear and unloving. Starting a business is not for everyone. It takes a lot of sacrifice and courage to put yourself out there, especially when there is no guarantee that your idea will pan out. To be a Black woman starting a business is extraordinary because these individuals face not only the barriers established by racism but also the pitfalls of patriarchy.

DeShuna Spencer, founder and CEO of kweliTV, a video streaming service that curates independent films, documentaries, and web series from the African diaspora, shares the challenges she encountered while financing her business in an interview with Kenrya Rankin in the book *How We Fight White Supremacy*. The Memphis native describes how she was able to get early rounds of funding through pitch and grant competitions, using an initial $20,000 she won in a competition to build the beta version of the platform. "Then it took two years to get out of beta," she shares. "That's a book within itself, the challenges of bootstrapping a company. I had no idea that Black women only get 0.2 percent of all venture capital investments until I was looking and saying, 'Where is the money?,' and people were saying, 'Good luck with that.' Technically, we're still a startup company, we're not fully funded. I'm doing this off blessings, holding it together with tears, bubble gum, and glue."[7]

Despite the odds working against them, Black women are creating businesses faster than any other demographic. During my research for the book, Black women told me that they launched their businesses because they wanted freedom and spaciousness in their lives. They have a vision of the type of person they want to be, the type of partner or friend they want to be, and the type of mother they want to be, and they see self-employment as the vehicle that can make it happen. It's about having command of one's schedule, work product, and environment that speaks to the abundance that Black women crave. The only problem, it turns out, is that business ownership means navigating capitalism. This is the Black entrepreneur's dilemma.

"When you have investors, they want to make a return in five years," Spencer shares in her conversation with Rankin. "Having an exit strategy essentially means selling your company to a Netflix or some other company that's not Black-owned. And if we want to continue to be a Black-owned company then we may not be able to take advantage of all the possible investment opportunities. I get emails from people saying, 'Don't become BET,' which means, 'Don't sell out.' But how do you reconcile that desire with the fact that one day you're going to have to sell it? That's something I am still trying to figure out."[8]

Running a successful business requires an ability to nurture the company, grow it, and keep it aligned with the original values. But it's difficult to maintain the vision of the company when it's not supported by the money. DeShuna Spencer's vision needs Believe-in-You Money. Without it, Black women and many others' desire for ownership over their life, their wealth, and their time is going to run headfirst into toxicity. Getting this right for women means that we get it right for everyone. Women are mothers, workers, and creators, and by centering their experiences, we can see and address the discrimination they face, which in turn sets us all up to succeed.

Unlocking Imagination and Creative Economy

Believe-in-You Money is for anyone supporting Black culture makers and creatives—women or otherwise—at a time when we deeply need to unlock our imagination in order to get an economy that loves Black people. One thing I know for sure is that if you want a loving economy (or anything at all), you have to be able to imagine it. That's why I love the question, What would it look like if the economy loved Black people? Answering it requires us to sit still and think about a world where we are loved. Admittedly, when I ask this question I am always met with a brief moment of naysaying and disbelief because it seems impossible to believe that we can ever have an economy that loves Black people. Not only do I believe that we can we have it, but I also believe it's inevitable. What we need to do now is imagine and act.

In a public conversation at the New School in 2015, bell hooks talked about moving from pain to power and said that if you can see life beyond the pain, then you can make a plan to get to the new vision. Having a plan is what separates fantasy from reality, and it's the active ingredient that makes our imagination come alive.[9] When we make a point to invest in Black creators and innovators, we are engaging in culture change work that incorporates imagination and action and challenges our current reality. By deepening our commitment to culture workers—using new tools for finance that bring antiracist and nonextractive capital experiences forward—we are transforming pain into the power needed to change the world.

Believe-in-You Money is the type of capital that best supports culture workers as they serve as the spokespersons and collaborators of the world, using their voices and energy to shape the future. When the world was falling apart in the early days of the pandemic, I tapped into D-Nice's DJ sessions and met my friends in the virtual streets to party and dance the night away. It was Verzuz, an American musical webcast series created by record producers Timbaland and Swizz Beatz, that carried us forward with a sense of community and reminded us that we are more than the current moment, and that together we would survive. Looking back, Black creatives are the ones who have been holding us emotionally and spiritually all along, and they need a return on their investment in the form of a changed system that unlocks restorative, liberating capital.

Changing Practices and Policies

Last but not least, *Believe-in-You Money* focuses on changing practices and policies of the funding process. Don't get me wrong—we need more Black leadership at all levels, from fund managers to boards of directors, because Black leadership matters. But this alone does not change the practices that keep wealth from reaching Black people more broadly. Only policy can do that. In fact, relying on Black leadership alone can mask the persistent racial inequality that still thrives in our society today. To restore wealth, we need investments that build political and economic power and move in tandem with the work of culture makers. This book establishes that the baseline of successfully moving resources to Black founders should, at a minimum, use the six guiding values.

CHAPTER 1

Believe-in-You Money

The first time I used the term "Believe-in-You Money" was during a keynote session I was facilitating for a conference on local economies in Cincinnati, Ohio. It was November 2015, and snow was coming down heavily. I opened the session with a story about the city's Black business legacy. I believe in calling on the histories of Black business owners as a way of acknowledging the long-standing legacy of and fight for equal opportunity. Their life stories provide me with language that enables me to give voice to the problems that Black owners face in service of moving forward. As you read this book, you'll encounter stories that animate the experiences of Black entrepreneurs. In my keynote speech that day in Cincinnati, I told the story of Henry Boyd.

Henry Boyd was born an enslaved person on a Kentucky plantation in 1802.[1] When he was 24, he arrived in Cincinnati, a free state, as a skilled carpenter and woodworker. Hoping to find work, he applied for jobs but was turned down when White workers threatened to leave if Boyd was hired. One day, when one of the White carpenters came to work drunk, Boyd took on the work and impressed the owner. Soon, he was contracted for more projects, and word began to spread about Boyd's talent. Over time, Boyd made enough money to purchase the freedom of his brother and sister.

With a growing number of customers, Boyd purchased a woodworking shop and began creating a new design for a bed frame, the Boyd Bedstead. The beds were sturdy and had railing that was both decorative and functional. But because of racial discrimination, he was unable to get a patent for his design. In 1833, a White cabinetmaker named George Porter was issued the patent for Boyd's designs. It's not known if Porter and Boyd worked together to secure the patent, but we do know that Boyd was a unique businessman. The H. Boyd Company was integrated with both White and Black men working together, and his popularity was such that prominent Cincinnatians of the time purchased his bed frames.

By 1855, the H. Boyd Company had expanded to include a showroom and took up several storefronts downtown. However, Boyd's vision of a fully integrated company was not welcomed by everyone. His business was burned down twice, and in 1862—with no companies willing to insure him—Boyd closed his doors for good. Despite being well known in abolitionist circles for his contributions as a conductor on the Underground Railroad, Boyd died with no remarkable fanfare and was buried in an unmarked grave.[2]

When I stepped offstage after sharing the story of Henry Boyd, Oscar Perry Abello, a journalist who covers local economics and power building, asked me what made me share Boyd's story. I told him that what happened to Boyd—the economic discrimination and violence—is still happening to Black companies today. Part of the reason for this is the persistent discrimination that created and continues to expand the wealth gap. Oscar and I talked about the ongoing sabotage that these owners are subjected to, often over many generations. "How do you change that?" he asked. I said, "We need to invest as if we care about the people and about the places they come from. We need Believe-in-You Money."

A few months after this exchange, Oscar published a story about my efforts to provide friendly, nonexploitative capital to Black founders as a form of repair for the racial discrimination they continue to face. When the piece went to print, I didn't yet have the language to name precisely what I was calling for. But over time I arrived at the term "Believe-in-You Money" to describe my proposal for a new approach that provides business capital in a way that can support the repair of racial injustice.

What Is Believe-in-You Money?

Believe-in-You Money is nonextractive,
patient capital that is explicitly antiracist.

It is not "venture capital, but make it Black." Believe-in-You Money is something different. It's community centered, rooted in storytelling and rituals of care and kinship. This kind of money is held by women in small villages in El Salvador as well as by giving circles in Birmingham, Alabama. This money is everywhere. The people who move this money are in sou sous, which are informal savings communities throughout the African diaspora, online on crowdfunding sites, in boardrooms, or sitting with their wealth manager. This money is drawn to the power of the people. This money makes you feel good. This money makes you feel seen. This money finds joy in the success of others. This money sees our shared humanity. This kind of money is an energy—the *Ase* of life itself—and has been moving between peoples for a millennium.

Believe-in-You Money is a commitment to providing Black founders and creators flexible, nonburdensome money at the beginning of their capital experience. It could be considered an intentional alternative to conventional friends-and-family capital because it's explicitly antiracist and nonextractive, but the spirit of the idea is the same. Believe-in-You Money can be in the form of gifts, grants, patient debt, revenue share, convertible equity, and other forms I have not thought of. The goal of the capital is to shift power and to build trust, mutual support, and respect.

Believe-in-You Money is the answer when we want to pour into one another in a way that provides an additional source of power to move forward. Perhaps you have received this kind of money or just instinctively understand the intentions. Believe-in-You Money is capital that is nonextractive; patient, long-term; and antiracist. These descriptors are discussed below.

1. Nonextractive

    Nonextractive capital broadly represents the belief that the money invested should benefit the founders more than the investor. Nonextractive terms can show up inside of the terms of repayment, interest rates, and risk management. Nonextractive finance can be used in loans, licensing, or royalty or future sales so long as the funds do not require the founder to give up equity. Nonextraction also means that repayment happens only when the company is able to cover operating expenses and when the business owner is able to pay themselves. In a nonextractive deal, security is based on the mission alignment and business preparedness of the company and a person's relationships with the community instead of collateral or personal assets. Finally, and most importantly, nonextractive capital does not use credit scores but rather uses a character-based underwriting process that looks at multiple dimensions of the company and the company's impact in the community.

2. Patient, Long-Term

    There are many funds that already use patient or long-term capital strategies. In *The Nature of Investing: Resilient Investment Strategies through Biomimicry*, Katherine Collins talks about how biomimicry—applying the wisdom of nature to human systems—can inform our investing decisions.[3] When we think about it, nature takes time to replenish and regenerate from a harvest or a major change in the environment, and if one were investing with nature, the return rate would be much slower, more harmonious, and interconnected to the people and the planet. These ideas are not new; they have been a part of Afro-Indigenous culture for a long time.

In the impact investing space, patient capital is often described as waiting a considerable amount of time—sometimes 10 years—before seeing a financial return. The idea behind patient capital is that by forgoing a quick return, we will get better social and environmental impact. Both the racial equity fund at RSF Social Finance and international lender Acumen use patient capital as a tool to support their investments.[4] Investors use patient capital because they understand that these businesses have more barriers to overcome on their way to success. Funds that use long-term repayment schedules also tend to work in closer partnership with the business owner, providing technical support and access to key relationships and resources.

3. Antiracist

   If you haven't already, I strongly recommend you read *How to Be an Antiracist*, by Ibram X. Kendi, who reminds us that the opposite of "racist" isn't "not racist." It is "antiracist." Antiracism is all about the action that flows from the awareness of racism. In other words, now that you know about the racial wealth gap, what action are you going to take to dismantle it? Kendi says that to be an antiracist is to commit to undoing racism by constantly identifying it, describing it, and dismantling it. Believe-in-You Money puts this concept into motion by asking us to take action using different rules, procedures, and guidelines for investing in Black-founded start-up companies. Instead of being color-blind, we need to be explicitly antiracist. Kendi reminds us that there is no such thing as race-neutral or nonracist policy, and that in order to end the racial wealth gap, we will have to make policies that promote racial equity and are antiracist.

The 6 Characteristics of Believe-in-You Money

This book offers two pathways to ensure the success of Black business owners: one path to support personal change, and another path to ensure systems change. Personal change is about how we, the readers, can make changes in how we support Black companies. In the first half of the book, I share that if we want to help Black founders, we need to invest using nonextractive money, long-term money, and antiracist money. This kind of investment will have a personal impact on the founder that increases the possibility of their business surviving and thriving. It puts capital in their hands that's much more reparative than what the market generally provides. But it does not change the system. For that, we need to talk about the six ways Believe-in-You Money can support systemic change.

The second half of the book is dedicated to going beyond investing in a Black founder alone to investing in the sustainability of Black-owned businesses and the ecosystem broadly. Chapters 4 through 9 introduce the six characteristics that can guide investment strategy, build power, and increase wealth in Black communities, using Black business investing as a starting strategy. I think these guiding characteristics are what make the difference. The systems change work is at the heart of what this book is aiming for—a revolutionary change in how we finance Black companies.

These chapters talk about the underlying values of Believe-in-You Money. You will quickly notice that each characteristic is a direct challenge to our current extractive system, and that is on purpose. I want us to see the current system; I want us to see what I am asking us to leave behind; and I want us to see what I'm inviting us to step into. I am asking us to leave behind an extractive economy in favor of a more loving and restorative economy. Ultimately, this is about "how we show up." As you read, you may notice that some of the language will seem familiar, especially if you are in social justice movement spaces, because these characteristics are rooted inside those spaces too. I have learned to rely on the six characteristics in *Believe-in-You Money* as a compass on the road to repair. Working with these characteristics creates a new opportunity to be adaptive and unique—no more cookie-cutter ideas; this is about transformation.

In an effort to clearly articulate the characteristics of Believe-in-You Money and support greater understanding, I created the Believe-in-You Money Investing Chart, identifying the goals and attributes of Believe-in-You Money, contrasted with the symptoms of today's extractive investing practices.

This chart is at the heart of the changes we could see when we use the ideas found in *Believe-in-You Money*. Black-owned businesses don't need to be in a competition for scarce or time-sensitive funds; they need to be in community, with access to the financial support they need to thrive. True Believe-in-You Money follows those biblical words on love: love "believes all things."

Believe-in-You Money Investing Chart

Money That Loves Black People	Extractive Money
Transformational relationships	Transactional relationships
Shared risk and the profit and reward go to the folks who did the work	Risk-averse
	Lion's share of profits goes to investor
Restorative, mutually beneficial, accountable	Unequal power dynamics
Centering those harmed	Complicit in maintaining systems of oppression and harm
Promotes transparency and open communication	Promotes secrecy, opacity, and unnecessary complication
Confronts and releases shame and fear	
Impact made through interdependence, collective action, democratic processes	Emphasizes individualistic, going-it-alone bootstrapping approach and reinforces the myth of meritocracy
Regenerative, stable systems	Exploitative, unstable systems

Ask yourself whether your investments embody the identifiers from the chart:

1. **Transformational relationships**—Are we creating relationships that are based in truth-telling? Are we centering relationships that allow for transparency and vulnerability, learning and unlearning, and growth and education?

2. **Shared risk**—Are we recentering our understanding of risk by asking ourselves, What can't we lose? This question focuses us on the things that matter: the workers, community well-being, and the planet.

3. **Restorative and mutually beneficial**—Have we created a space that addresses power dynamics and differences? Are we centering the experience of the founder rather than that of the investor? What does this look like when we have created spaces and conditions that are restorative and reparative?

4. **Release shame and fear**—Can we invite healing into this process? Is there a pathway to be courageous and open with our concerns? Can we create spaciousness to invite clarity over complication? Can we relax some of our ideas of process-heavy workloads with good communication, transparency, and grace?

5. **Collective action**—What does this look like if we emphasize community over the ideas of a single leader, which leads to founder burnout? How does our strategy unlock more collective power?

6. **Regenerative systems**—Did we build an ecosystem of support around the company and the community? Did we honor the cultural relationships that call for intersectional thinking? Are we building systems that allow people to thrive and that create sustainable places?

This list of characteristics can help you identify places where you can check in and evaluate the work. Questions like "Does this investment support collective action?" will help us determine whether we are doing personal change or systems change. It's wise to revisit these concepts every so often to see if you are moving in alignment with your intentions. The truth is, we will need to be in process and in community about repairing racial harm for a lifetime. Just remember to embrace adaptation and give yourself grace. Remember that these six characteristics are about systems change, which is all about shifting attitudes, behaviors, and beliefs toward a new way of doing things. I am clear that I want to shift toward an economy that loves Black people. This is not Band-Aid work; if we commit to this, it will unlock and uplift the brilliance of Black people in a really special way.

In writing this book, I had the honor of talking to the legends in my life—leaders who manage funds, foundations, and financial institutions and who lead movements that build power and restore our soul. I spoke with seven friends, most of whom are Black women, with a White man and an Asian man in the mix too. Some of these individuals identify as queer. I asked them to talk to me about Believe-in-You Money in their lives, whether they've ever received this kind of support, and what it would mean to our community if others got it. We spent a lot of time talking candidly about race and power inside of money, with truth-telling as a recurring theme. I asked them what advice they would give to others who wanted to follow in their footsteps and invest Believe-in-You Money, and the answers were honest and profound. They all said in their own ways that we need to be doing our personal, internal work to undo racism in ourselves and in our systems. I am deeply grateful for the trust they have given me. Their ideas helped me understand what's possible and unpack what has been holding us back, offering space to see the intersections of our relationships with wealth and racial equity. Together, we lift up a vision of transformation so powerful that I wish for all of us to hear it, invest in it, and experience it.

CHAPTER 2

An Economy That Loves Black People

It was late March 2020, and I was sick in bed, convinced that every cough and every ache in my body was COVID-19. This particular night, I was clutching my chest, talking to God and my ancestors. As I floated someplace between here and not here, words emerged from my consciousness. In the dark, I wrote a question in my journal.

What would it look like if the economy loved Black people?

At the time—mere weeks into the ongoing coronavirus pandemic—over 40 percent of Black-owned businesses had closed. Most of those companies were in the retail, hospitality, and service industries, and many of them were led by women. Claire Mills of the New York Federal Reserve issued a report that investigated and elevated the pandemic's impact on Black-owned businesses. Mills reported that they "had weaker cash positions, weaker bank relationships, and pre-existing funding gaps prior to the pandemic." She further wrote, "COVID-19 has exacerbated these issues and businesses in the hardest-hit communities have witnessed huge disparities in access to federal relief funds and a higher rate of business closures."[1]

Amid this disruption, I shared my newfound question a few weeks later with my colleagues at the Center for Economic Democracy, at an event centered on the famous Grace Lee Boggs prompt, "What time is it on the world clock?" Each of the center's fellows gave context and meaning to what was happening in the world, from their own perspective. When it was my turn, I had only one question in my heart—a question that required both an inquiry of imagination and an acknowledgment that the current financial system has no love for Black people.

By this time, in this particular conversation and across all my work, this question—What would it look like if the economy loved Black people?—had become my anchor and my North Star that would lead me to the systemic change I dream of.

An Economy That Loves Black People?

I am really curious about the idea of having an economy that loves Black people. I love all the possibilities it unearths inside me, and that feels exciting and remarkable. I must admit that when I think about the question, I often find myself vacillating between "maybe it's possible" and "ain't no way." But always I am reminded that the answer to the question of what it would look like if the economy loved Black people is really up to each of us. The question is meant to invite imagination and curiosity that lead to a clear vision for a future that includes the systemically excluded. When I think about the question, I fixate on the word "love," because I know that love is about action. And instantly, the question becomes more personal, and I think, "What will *I* do?"

When I asked my friends featured in the book what they thought about it, we started to weave a tapestry of ideas that felt like fabric of the highest refinement. What would it look like if the economy loved Black people? Children would be fed, reading scores would skyrocket, housing stability would increase, prisons would close, Afro-Indigenous health and medicine would return, and more. I imagine it would feel like the curtains are pulled back, revealing a lush garden full of possibilities, dripping with honeysuckle and palm leaves, and a sky so blue that it looks like the ocean, a sea of possibilities that can carry you anywhere you want to go on its waves of promise. I imagine the way we are all loved—not for what we can do but for what we bring to the world. I imagine rest and peace and divine joy. I imagine a place for all people to thrive.

I hope this book inspires us to see that another way is possible, one that is in alignment with the people and places we care about. In this way, I hope the question inspires both the people who are moving capi- tal and Black business owners, all of whom can discover that other op- tions are available. I hope to convey that these ideas are not exclusively for the wealthy or the elite. In fact, it doesn't matter if you consider your- self wealthy or if that word doesn't align with how you see yourself in the world. What matters is that you are a part of a global community of people who are committed to investing in Black brilliance.

This committed community is operating inside of social impact spaces and philanthropy conferences, often meeting up in the hallways outside of sessions to talk about the investments they are making in racial justice. They are in investment clubs focused on funding for women, and they are part of global nongovernmental organizations doing mi- crofinance. This community of investors is growing, slowly but surely stretching into mainstream investing. Today may be about venture cap- ital, but tomorrow is all about community capital—capital that is non- extractive and founder centered and that imagines a joyful and humane world. This community of investors is transforming the ways we invest in Black people and places.

How the Question Has Guided Me

Around the same time my North Star question came into focus, RUN- WAY was working overtime to make sure the companies in our port- folio got Paycheck Protection Program (PPP) loans in light of the disruption the pandemic caused in their businesses and lives. In *Racial Dispari- ties in Paycheck Protection Program Lending*, the National Bureau of

Economic Research reported that Black-owned businesses were the least likely to receive PPP loans and that "subjectivity was most likely to influence lending decisions."[2] That's code for racism. This is particularly disturbing because the lenders faced no risk. The PPP was 100 percent guaranteed by the federal government.

I remember being in the depths of heartbreak after the murders of Breonna Taylor, Ahmaud Arbery, and George Floyd. But it was seeing George Floyd crying out for his mother that made the words come from my body in the way they did. I was seeking explanations for his death and found myself focused on the counterfeit $20 bill that was at the heart of the conflict. That fake currency opened my eyes to how fake all of it was—from the counterfeit bill to the entire system surrounding it. In the days after George Floyd's murder, we saw corporations and banks pledging their support to Black-owned businesses. It was dizzying, all of a sudden seeing everyone focused on Black founders. Why now? Why focus on Black founders now, when everything is so bad?

Looking back to the civil rights era gives us some understanding of what the response was all about. This form of bait and switch was a bastion of President Richard Nixon's Southern Strategy, a plan that sought to pacify White Americans and crush Black American political power building. In an article in the *New York Times* on April 26, 1968, Nixon shared his "new approach" for the nation's racial problems. "What the militants are asking for," he said, "is not separation but to be included not as supplicants, but as owners, as entrepreneurs—to have a share of the wealth, a piece of the action."[3] Nixon's agenda of Black capitalism became an effective tool to quell the impacts of a powerful civil rights movement.

By allowing Black communities to use their own money to create a "beneficial multiplier effect," the theory went, Black-owned businesses and Black banking would be the key to Black economic progress. This move satisfied the White conservative base who opposed demands for reparations, integration, and even equal resources for schools. While a generation of White Americans gained wealth through welfare programs sponsored by the federal government, like credit subsidies for student and mortgage loans, Nixon wanted Black people to use the free market. "For too long," Nixon said, "White America has sought to buy off its own sense of guilt with ever more programs of welfare, of public housing, of payments to the poor."[4] By discouraging welfare dependency in the name of "Black enterprise," he was able to undermine Black demands for economic redress and reparations. Today, this idea is behind efforts like "enterprise zones," "new market tax credits," "promise zones," and "opportunity zones."[5] These programs fail to provide the meaningful financial support that Black communities ask for, instead becoming Band-Aid solutions that lack the fundamental change needed to overcome our country's legacy of slavery and racial exclusion.

As the calls continued to ring out for support of Black-owned businesses in light of antiracist uprisings happening across the globe in the summer of 2020, I held true to the fact that there has never been an intentional pathway for Black wealth building in this nation that was not later receded and reneged: 40 acres and a mule, the GI Bill, and countless other efforts to build Black wealth in America have been burned to the ground and bulldozed by urban renewal programs and racism. The question of an economy that loves Black people got more real for me in the aftermath of George Floyd's death.

What is Love? Love is a Verb.

—bell hooks

Inspired by the words of feminist scholar bell hooks, I think of love the way she described it, as "a combination of care, commitment, knowledge, responsibility, respect and trust."[6] It is the action of love that I find most compelling as a salve to the wounds of racism. Admittedly, when people hear me talk about love as a tool for repair, they roll their eyes and grunt under their breath. They are skeptical that love is a real strategy for change, and I can understand why. Love is subjective. hooks said, "We do not have to love. We **choose** to love. . . . When we understand love as the will to nurture our own and another's spiritual growth, it becomes clear that we cannot claim to love if we are hurtful and abusive. Love and abuse cannot coexist."[7] I choose love because there can be no justice without love. I choose love because there is no truth-telling without love. I choose love because it is the foundation upon which we can see ourselves truly and accept ourselves so that we can reconnect with self and one another in a repaired and renewed space.

In the fallout of the pandemic, our team at RUNWAY responded to our portfolio's urgent and complex needs in the image of an economy that loves Black people. We were watching all these other folks take a left turn, approaching Black founders and putting them in more and more stress, with more paperwork to fill out, more questions to answer, more requirements to meet. We went the other direction. In the interest of creating ease, we provided RUNWAY businesses with flexible capital and the freedom and flexibility to self-determine how they spent it—we created our own universal basic income program.

Universal basic income (UBI) is an ongoing, direct cash payment—free of burdensome administrative requirements or other spending restrictions—that acknowledges that people know how to best meet their own needs, and simply need the resources and freedom to do so. RUNWAY's UBI pilot was the first in the nation to specifically address the economic inequality of Black founders. We told our founders that we would pay them $1,000 per month for six months to support them and their families during COVID. I remember gathering on the phone with the entire RUNWAY team and our portfolio of companies as the first payments began arriving in May 2020. Each person spoke, and soon we were all in tears. Nobody on the call had ever experienced what we were experiencing, and it was fundamentally changing us for the better.

Looking back, the benefits of this type of investment were clear. Having cash in hand changed everything for the business owners. Ninety-eight percent of our companies remained open during the pandemic, beating the national average. We often talk about how important relationships are for a business, and this is when those relationships really mattered. We know that when a business owner has a well-resourced network, that owner can weather the storms that come their way. We also know that, because of the racial wealth gap, Black founders typically do not have the kinds of networks with resources that can help them in financially stressful times. RUNWAY understood this and we did what we knew would matter: we showed up in love. This is what Believe-in-You Money is all about.

The Economy We Have

For the past 20 years, the financial field has been saying that "access to capital" for Black companies is a clear problem. Yet the fundamentals of how Black companies access capital have not changed. Black business owners are still more likely to be denied credit and they still pay higher interest rates than White business owners. As a result, fewer Black entrepreneurs apply for loans. Black founders are so underfunded that they are tapping retirement accounts, credit cards, and emergency savings—all very costly ways to access capital. Black entrepreneurs need a robust friends-and-family round of capital. For many entrepreneurs, this abundant, flexible, and no- to low-risk pool of capital is a financial lifeline that can be the difference between a promising idea and a successfully launched start-up.

That is, unless you're Black.

As I shared in the introduction, Black families have $11,000 in net worth, while White American families have $141,900. And since we live in a largely segregated society, in which systems and structures divide wealth along racial lines and the average person's network is not demographically diverse, the great ideas of many Black entrepreneurs never leave the napkin. Their networks simply can't provide the funds to launch a business. This only compounds into a credit gap for Black entrepreneurs.

Today, only 1 percent of venture-backed businesses are Black owned. Since there's no clear process to understand how investors make investment decisions, trying to get a meeting is often a mysterious and unsuccessful venture. Even in the relatively rare occasion that a Black founder gets a meeting, they often must jump through additional hoops to prove that they have the same credentials as another CEO who might fit a more stereotypical founder profile. Most investors (banks, angels, venture capitalists, community development financial institutions, foundations) share a mind-set about investing in Black firms that comes from what they think they know about "diversity," which is generally insufficient and inaccurate. In part because of this disconnect, their strategies often downplay the reality that the demographics of the market have shifted and that the data confirms that investing in Black-owned businesses is a powerful strategy for delivering returns.

The conversation about Black-owned businesses as a solution dates back to at least the 1950s, and the denial of business opportunities to Black Americans has been happening since the country's origins. What is now often referred to as the racial wealth gap is the result of historical harms and terroristic policies. There's a gap, but it didn't simply appear; it was created by redlining, lynching, extractive financing, mass incarceration, and more. It's long past time to acknowledge the cumulative impact that racism continues to have on Black wealth building.

Continuing to promote the idea that Black founders can bootstrap their way out of the racial wealth gap is reckless. It turns a blind eye to the very real systemic barriers that often make bootstrapping impossible for individual Black founders. Black founders deserve capital that transforms their relationship to finances and benefits their family's relationship to money for generations to come. We need practices that are grounded in traditions that honor Black culture in its fullness, not ones that only offer inclusion into a racist system, in exchange for contorting ourselves into structures that don't fit us.

Now is the time to interrupt the historical harm and offer an alternative that nurtures Black wealth. We need Believe-in-You Money, reparative capital that values all people and life; centers Afro-Indigenous values of restoration; and practices community governance, shared risk, and ownership. We can show love to Black people by using Believe-in-You Money to invest in Black entrepreneurs with powerful, innovative ideas. Our responsibility to one another, as people who understand our interconnectedness, is to work to shift our economy from an extractive one to one that creates more justice, equity, and healing. It's time to earn money differently, spend money differently, and grow money differently. Our nation is in need of much healing, especially when it comes to racism and the harm caused by racism that remains embedded in our financial systems. Together, we can change these systems.

Believe-in-You Money Is Changing Things

One of the first things that Believe-in-You Money does is invite and encourage investments that eliminate systemic racism from lending practices, and that can lead to a transformation of the way capital moves. Our current economy has made only small-scale, surface, and/or conditional and extractive investments in Black business owners. To close the wealth gap, larger, deeper, and more trusting and generous investments must become the standard. Kate Poole, an investor and next economy wealth adviser, shares how she found her way to transformational lending by way of a Believe-in-You Money approach: "I was struck by a contradiction in my own work—*I realized that, while I was donating money to Black-led organizing for Black liberation, I wasn't giving money to investment projects working to build intergenerational Black wealth.* I decided to give RUNWAY more money than I'd ever given to one organization at a time before, $20,000."[8]

I love what Kate shared because it was an aha moment that caused a ripple effect and increased the depth and reach of her investments and impact. Believe-in-You Money invites us to reach beyond the surface and transform the system. By using Believe-in-You Money, we are following a systems-change approach to address the erasure of Black contributions, stolen Black labor, and the unseen glass ceiling of wealth, instead investing in Black prosperity, now and in the future. What those of us who believe in Believe-in-You Money are asking is for people to *believe* that there is a way to a better, more equitable future in this country. To believe that there is something better for us collectively. To believe that healing is available. And to put our resources, our hearts, our whole bodies and selves behind that belief. Even given our fraught history of racism and extraction from Black people and communities, and even though we don't have proof that it could change, we have faith that better is possible.

The emotions we witnessed during the RUNWAY UBI launch brought to life the power of Believe-in-You Money. I will never forget the words of one of the founders: "You've done more for me, my family, and my community and this business than the federal government has done." And at that point in time, it was true.

RUNWAY is just one organization; imagine what we could do to-gether. With this book, I'm doing my best to share all that I know about Believe-in-You Money. I hope that it becomes a guide for you or an inspi-ration. However you choose to engage with the material, I hope you will remember that we do not have to live like this. We can invest in a way that is more just and changes the systemic issues around investing in Black founders.

The COVID pandemic inspired many people to imagine what might come after such an immense world event, and I've heard many people say, "We will return, but I don't see us returning to normal." Who wants to go back to normal? I think of Sonya Renee Taylor, whom you'll hear from in the next chapter, who reminds us that normal never was. To-gether, we can make love, healing, and justice the new normal.

CHAPTER 3

Antiracist Investors

The number of people moving money in ways that align with their values about racial justice and equity is growing. They might be pooling money to get the owner of the local bakery up and running, using their money to keep the doors open at the Black-owned bookstore that's been in the community for over 50 years, or supporting local Black food producers by prepaying for fruits and vegetables in order to give them the cash needed to plant and grow for the upcoming season.

I have witnessed these people come together in giving circles, inside of sou sous and investment circles. I have watched them connect on threads on social media platforms in order to donate to something important, like helping a business owner reopen after a fire. I have seen a person move their personal money into a community-owned grocery store, and I have seen a fund manager invest in a company that finds cures for diseases that disproportionately affect Black and Indigenous communities, like heart disease and hypertension.

Here's the thing: this group of people may not self-define as investors.

But if you think of investing as more than large financial investments, many more people fit the description of "investor." People who invest their time, their talents, and their money into creating a more just world are all investing in different ways. From my perspective, anyone who uses their resources to create a world that loves Black people is an antiracist investor.

One of the things that tie this community together is their commitment to doing the personal work to transform racism in their lives and in the systems operating around them. Ruth King, who teaches transformational courses on mindfulness and racism, uses language I really appreciate: "Transform racism from the inside out."[1] King talks about the connection between how we think and how we respond that sits at the core of both the suffering and the healing of racism.[2] This community of wealth movers and wealth holders believes that, through personal change work (how we think) and systemic change work (how we respond), we can ultimately end systemic racism and restore our humanity.

In addition to Ruth King, experts such as Konda Mason and Anu Gupta—whose voices are featured throughout this book—similarly use their mindfulness practices to anchor their antiracism work. Taking a note from these leaders, I've engaged mindfulness-based meditation to help me move from the distress of racism back into compassion and curiosity with myself and others. The practice has offered me a pathway into a more grounded, strategic, and intentional way of moving when I am confronted with harmful and violent systems of oppression.

Working first on the inner self, antiracist investors understand how crucial it is to unpack their personal trauma as a prerequisite to any attempts to dismantle systemic racism. The importance of working on oneself in order to transform the economy is at the heart of Believe-in-You Money. Concepts like truth-telling and transformation echo throughout the pages. I remember asking a friend who manages a fund in the style of Believe-in-You Money what makes someone say yes to investing practices that center racial justice and equity, and she said, without skipping a beat, "They're doing their personal work to undo racism." This personal work is foundational to systems change, and we cannot create liberated systems if we haven't tapped into the power of liberating ourselves. I think we forget that systems are made of people and that if we want the system to change, we need the people to change. Working from the inside out, as King suggests, is how we get meaningful and powerful change.

Decolonized Thinkers

I've noticed that this community is talking about decolonizing everything—including money. They're looking at ways to stop the cycles of harm and trauma that have indoctrinated our psyches and our systems as a result of colonization. To decolonize is to restore the freedom and self-determination that were stripped from Afro-Indigenous people through the colonial project. It means respecting Afro-Indigenous people and other historically subjugated people's ways of being and doing; it means respecting their cultures and customs without infringing on them. It requires what Toni Morrison invited us to do: move beyond the "White gaze," where Whiteness is the default lens that we use to see the world and ourselves. It demands that we shift the power imbalance that continues to maintain colonial dynamics.

There are so many ways to think about decolonization—as it relates to our homes, educational institutions, the health-care system, how we grow and consume our food, and, of course, our relationships with money. *Believe-in-You Money* looks expressly at the grip colonialism has on our money relationships. Author and philanthropist Edgar Villanueva is one of the key actors advancing the movement to decolonize banking, investment, finance, philanthropy, and every wealth center connected to them with his calls to action to use money as medicine to heal from the "colonizer virus."[3] Regardless of the field or industry in focus, the central point of decolonization is the belief that we can be a healthier, safer, and more connected people if we leave our exploitative past behind by doing the difficult work of confronting and transforming the wounds.

Decolonized thinking creates a future where Black people thrive. In this future, we reject rigidity and the false separation established by colonial perspectives. We embrace fluidity and accept that nothing is fixed, stationary, or binary, but rather, the challenges we face are intersectional, and we must identify solutions that are adaptable and that honor intersectionality. By embracing complexity and acknowledging that no two people or situations are the same, fluidity invites much more flexibility. This flexibility comes as a result of the curiosity and compassion we can tap into when we commit to mindfulness.

Intersectional Thinkers

As intersectional thinkers, antiracist investors understand that race, gender, and class are never separate; they are keenly aware of the ways that these forms of power can collide with one another causing both harm and injustice. In the words of Kimberlé Crenshaw, the lawyer and professor who coined the term "intersectionality," "It's not simply that there's a race problem here, a gender problem here, and a class or LBGTQ problem there. Many times that framework erases what happens to people who are subject to all of these things."[4] Intersectional perspectives understand that racial, socioeconomic, health, and political disparities are more pervasive for marginalized people and communities. The intersection of racial and/or class and/or gender identity marginalization shapes the lived experiences of Black woman entrepreneurs, for instance, who are navigating many identities and challenging conventional structural inequities just by being women running their own companies. Things like whether a woman has a supportive partner to carry family responsibilities while she grows her business can intersect with the additional burden she faces when entering the marketplace. Given the patriarchal culture we live in, men often start out with fewer barriers outside of the workplace, giving them an edge because they can dedicate more of themselves to their companies.

In addition to honoring intersectionality, antiracist investors also believe in interconnectedness. They see how the systems and institutions around them routinely marginalize specific populations while continually privileging others, ultimately creating divisions between and among us. These people recognize that the systems are operating by design and that the only way to stop the damage they're doing is to attack them at their core. These systems could then be replaced with new ones that reclaim Afro-Indigenous culture and center interrelatedness as opposed to separateness and competition. This group hungers to revive and center ancestral language, behavior, customs, knowledge, symbols, ideas, values, and spirit in order to provide a healthier design for living with and relating to one another that allows more people to lead safe and joyful lives. The Zulu word *ubuntu*, contemporarily popularized by South African archbishop Desmond Tutu, means "I am because we are" or "humanity toward others." A deep sense of all of us belonging to a human race is the guiding light that antiracist investors are following.

Courageous Thinkers

I've also noticed a common behavior among the antiracist investor community of reading and talking about courage and vulnerability. They know that challenging the system takes courage, especially when it comes to talking about themselves and their own difficult experiences with racism and money. They find kinship with the work of Brené Brown and resonance in her definition of vulnerability—moving with uncertainty, taking risks, and opening up emotionally—as a measure of their courage. Because they are willing to let go of comfort and ego in order to create spaces of safety and equitable coexistence with other people, antiracist investors are early adopters of transformational change-making ideas.

Not only do courage and vulnerability invite one's whole heart into everything they do and welcome others to do the same, but they also change the power dynamic. At the heart of it all, antiracist investors are committed to dismantling oppressive power structures everywhere. They are working to end oppression in the workplace, in schools, in the home, and—most fundamentally—within themselves. They understand the ways that oppressive power structures have made it hard for people who have experienced injustice to be fully present and engaged members of a community, and they know that creating conditions to be present and engaged is essential and foundational to any potential progress toward their vision of decolonized systems.

Choosing to speak up instead of remaining silent is what antiracist investors do best. By remaining collectively quiet about the oppressions that people are experiencing, we allow those with systemic power and privilege to hide and deny the reality. But by moving with courage, antiracist investors are able to initiate meaningful actions that interrupt the exclusion of others and stop the replication of operations and policies that continue to maintain control over the wealth, resources, and mobility of marginalized communities. Antiracist investors are on the front lines of environmental, gender, and resource justice issues all over the world.

Antiracist investors know that race is a construct—there is only one human race—but they are not color-blind. They understand the lies behind the racial categories created in service of extraction, colonialism, and capitalism and see the very real ways that the idea of White superiority has shaped our senses of self, our histories, and our political and economic frameworks and rewards those who align the privileges of ease, normality, and safety with it.

Antiracist investors want to end the routine exclusion of Black and Indigenous people from financing by conventional investors, venture capital firms, and commercial banks. They are both wealth holders and wealth movers. They are business owners who remember what it's like to get started. They are activists who are shaping the public consciousness. They are employees who are pushing their companies to go beyond diversity, equity, and inclusion and move into explicitly antiracist policy and culture. They are the customers and champions of Black and Brown brands.

A common characteristic of this group of people is their belief in the power of community. They believe that a healed world is possible when we commit to working in community. The provocative question "What does it mean to be a good ancestor?" was popularized by philosopher Roman Krznaric in his book *The Good Ancestor: A Radical Prescription for Long-Term Thinking*. If we want to be good ancestors and remembered as such by the generations who follow us, now is the time to recover and enrich the skills needed to leave society better than we found it.[5] The richness and ripple effect of Krznaric's work are felt inside organizations like Good Ancestor Movement, which was founded by Stephanie Brobbey, a UK-based private wealth lawyer and adviser who is helping individuals and organizations bring wealth redistribution and liberation together in order to advance social equity, economic justice, and ecological resistance.[6]

Characteristics of an Antiracist Investor

Antiracist investors are

- dismantling racism, personally and systemically, from the inside out, using mindfulness meditation, literature, training sessions, or study groups, all around the world.
- decolonizing everything in their lives—from the foods they eat to the ways they use their money—in an effort to shift the power imbalances that maintain colonial rule and power and to restore Afro-Indigenous freedom and self-determination.
- thinking at the intersections of race, gender, and class in a way that understands that these identities are never separate from our experience with institutions of power and that often they collide in pervasive ways for marginalized people and communities creating multiple layers of injustice and inequality.
- clear that racism is a construct and that we are human beings, interconnected by the same thread of life. As people who acknowledge

and honor interconnectedness, they are led by the Zulu word *ubuntu* ("I am because we are" or "humanity toward others").

- bringing courage and vulnerability to the table, speaking up against racism rather than remaining quiet, and practicing radical compassion for all people around the world.

An Antiracist's View on Return on Investment

From teachers to business owners to everyday community members, anyone investing in Black and Brown people and places in order to create positive outcomes is an antiracist investor. For people following this intentional approach, a return on investment doesn't have to be money alone; social and environmental returns matter just as much as financial profits.

In the Triple Bottom Line framework, established by John Elkington for measuring corporate performance, investment returns are viewed through their social and environmental impact in addition to their financial impact. These more holistic returns are sometimes called the 3Ps: people, planet, and profits. The idea is that investors are interested in positive returns among the people, the planet, and finally, their profits. If I were to update this measurement using an antiracist lens, I would call it the 4Ps, adding political returns to focus on the political power that affected communities amass as a result of investment and business growth.

When thinking of returns this way, investing becomes a powerful tool for aligning beliefs and actions in service of equity and justice. This type of impact goes beyond shareholder return and requires that the people and places surrounding that business see a return on the investment. Imagine if owners of a factory or plant considered the impact of its operations on workers or on the groundwater or on health, wellness, and safety when getting investment capital. It would be game changing. This is the kind of thinking that underpins Believe-in-You Money, the understanding that return on investment can be imagined in many ways other than what our current dominant system acknowledges, and repairing financial malpractice and injustice can be a measure of return too.

Where to Find Antiracist, Believe-in-You Money Investors

Organizations, companies, and investors that are committed to Black-owned businesses and minority-owned entities are naturally connected to the concepts of Believe-in-You Money. They are working on the ground and know how valuable and transformational this type of money can be for a business's bottom line, so they are often connecting with resource providers like RUNWAY or even making Believe-in-You Money available through their own funds and grant making.

Other likely places you'll find antiracist investors include the following:

- **Historically Black colleges and universities**
- **Centers for entrepreneurship at university business schools**
- **Nonprofit business accelerators**
- **Community development financial institutions**
- **Credit unions or banks** that pledge to increase diversity
- **Arts and culture spaces** prioritizing the wealth building and equity of Black artists and culture workers
- **Racial equity conferences** working to shift a company's or organization's internal culture, policy, and purchasing practices from the inside out
- **Social justice circles** organizing workers and neighbors, registering voters, building community funds, fighting for human rights and the protection of land, and uplifting the young people around them
- **Regenerative investing scene** (sometimes called impact investing) focused on B Corps, Web3, and blockchains, business impact

for the social good, Indigenous lessons about wealth, and a generally greater well-being among humanity

- **Faith-based communities** aligning their resources with the principles of their faith, beloved community, and resistance to oppression

There are many existing examples of how antiracist investors embody a Believe-in-You Money approach. The conversations and motivations among these antiracist investors are all a little bit different too. To give you a glimpse into the types of situations and circumstances that they face, I offer a few examples of Believe-in-You Money investors:

- **Terry is the head of investing for the Office of the Comptroller.** Terry wants to make investments in Black companies in his city, but he has to get his team and the advisory board—all former bankers and not very open to innovation—to approve his deals. He is using public dollars and needs to be prudent, but he also needs to make a big impact. Terry has been using Believe-in-You Money to guide his stakeholders in the hopes that this will lead to more internal support for investing in Black-owned businesses.
- **Rebecca works for her family's high-end coffee import business.** The company has been around for over 200 years and was once active in colonial control in the Caribbean. With history coming into public view more clearly, Rebecca wants to use the company's position to invest in Black woman coffee producers. She talked to her wealth manager, who advised her that if she wants to do good, she should invest in an environmental portfolio instead. Rebecca felt defeated. She's using the ideas of Believe-in-You Money to guide her conversations with her dad, the owner of the company, to encourage him to invest in a supply chain of Black woman

producers. She is also sharing her ideas with her wealth manager so that they can dig deeper to find investment opportunities that she can get behind.

- **James is an entrepreneur who owns a high-end men's clothing line in a historically Black enclave.** He is doing really well, but he sees the decline of the neighborhood where his shop is located. He would love to help in some way. So far, he's organized a community cleanup of vacant lots and worked with the city to remove absentee landlords from the area. James has gotten a lot of people excited and would like to use the momentum to fill the vacant locations with businesses run by people from the community. James does not see himself as an investor. He thinks his time spent cleaning up the neighborhood and organizing for more business is just charity. But regardless of the language he's using, he is definitely investing time and money to help support more Black companies.

- **Shawn owns a music accelerator where he rents studio space and helps musicians develop their projects.** The business is growing, especially on the studio and venue rental side. Instead of hiring staff, Shawn asked a graduate of the accelerator, Sonya, to manage the day-to-day operations of the building. With the contract, Sonya was able to get some monthly capital coming into her event management business. She was also able to list a new client—the music accelerator—which helped her gain two more venue management contracts. Shawn wouldn't say that he's an investor. He thinks that working with Sonya is just the right thing to do. He would be surprised to learn that this kind of investing has created a real opportunity for Sonya's business, one that may otherwise not have happened without an investor like Shawn.

- **Lynda is a college law professor with a best-selling book.** She's from a low-income background, and her newfound success has made her the backbone of her family, both financially and emotionally. Her mom lives with her, and her younger sister, who has two small children, needs money for living and educational expenses. To help her sister, Lynda gave her the money she needed for dental hygienist classes. But with the class load, Lynda's sister is asking for more help with the children. Lynda and her mom decide to take the younger children in, temporarily, while Lynda's sister finishes school. Lynda is not an investor in the conventional sense, yet she made an investment in her sister's dreams, stability, and ability to provide for herself and her family in the future.

Antiracist investors are thoughtful, courageous, and values-driven people who intentionally use the wealth they steward to dismantle the barriers that Black founders face because of deep-seated, systemic racial discrimination. By investing their resources in Black brilliance, imagination, and joy, they are creating a more equitable and regenerative future for all.

CHAPTER 4

Transformational versus Transactional Relationships

Having an experience like getting the capital you need, when you need it, in a way that is generous, loving, and thoughtful can alter your life and affect you in such a way that you are forever changed. That's what this chapter is all about: the deep, soul-changing transformation that is needed in order to truly encourage and support Black-owned companies. Among the many shifts needed in order to reshape experiences and outcomes for Black business owners and for *all* Americans, we need a transformation that fundamentally changes economic structures and systems. This is what Believe-in-You Money calls for: the kind of transformation that establishes equitable access to capital for Black founders and guides our collective in the direction of closing the racial wealth gap for good. We can't get to this transformation with the type of transactional relationships that currently dominate the financial system.

Transactional relationships perpetuate secrets and shame, which I talk more about in chapter 7, and keep us feeling like we are strangers to one another when we want—and need—to feel like a community. Transactional relationships maintain the status quo; they strip us of opportunities for meaning making and learning from and with one another. Relating to each other transactionally makes it hard for us to collectively understand or navigate complexity or adversity, which we need to do in order to grow or improve. The promise of transactional relationships is that both parties get something of value from the other. But if you read the fine print, the party with the most power always determines the value. A transactional relationship does not require morals, values, or principles—good or otherwise. Instead, transactional relationships maintain the existing set of imbalanced and inequitable processes and structures that govern our institutions and dealings with one another, continuing to divide rather than unite us.

At RUNWAY, we create transformational relationships with financial providers and community-led groups in order to bring more innovative capital solutions for Black companies to the marketplace. We are committed to creating holistic interventions that center entrepreneurs instead of being driven by investors and centering their needs. To honor the RUNWAY vision of transformation, we are anchored by a funders' manifesto that helps us connect with mission-aligned investors and fuels our work in equitable ways. The manifesto is the brainchild of our investing and development director, Alicia DeLia. Alicia is an economist and experienced development professional with decades of experience raising capital for investment strategies in Africa and North America. Alicia guides our work with the principle that capital can be used to heal, repair, and connect Black-owned businesses and the communities surrounding them. This principle informs all aspects of our organizational culture, from our lending and credit processes with our entrepreneurs to the interpersonal working relationships within our team and with our financial and banking partners.[1]

Building a transformational relationship takes work and patience. Early on in the COVID-19 pandemic, we found ourselves on the phone with our banking partner advocating for six months of deferred payments for our portfolio of companies. Instead, they offered their regular "disaster" package of three months of deferred payments. We were stuck and had not reached an agreement when the meeting ended. Negotiations spilled onto the email thread where we kept insisting that the deferment needed to be longer in order for the support to make a difference. Finally, the bank partner conceded.

We thought we were in the clear when another problem arose. The bank partner wanted the entrepreneurs to call in every month and request the deferment. We pushed back. Requiring entrepreneurs to call every month, while navigating all the challenges of a pandemic, created a scenario where the founder would always feel uncertain about the support, which would ultimately affect their ability to plan ahead. On top of that, it would make an already stressful situation even more stressful.

It seemed like we were stuck again. After many, many conversations, we began to understand that the bank partner didn't want to burden the business owners with the requirement to call in every month for an extension, but that the program—the actual system used to make deferments—only had a one-month option button. It turns out that we needed to change the button. Several engineers and designers had to be brought in to add this feature to the computer system, but the adoption of the button was and is transformational, because together we changed the systems of operation toward racial equity. This example also highlights how crucial it is to consider every element of our systems, because even something seemingly minor can cause damaging inequities.

I think the value we place on transformational relationships over transactional ones is one of the things that make RUNWAY unique. We use our manifesto not only as a way of grounding ourselves as a partner but also as an invitation to mission-aligned investors to support our work by learning more about our values and culture with respect to investing, philanthropy, and equitable partnerships. The manifesto and all the other measures we build into our process systemically support us in seeing the wholeness of all the people in our ecosystem—bankers and business owners alike. We honor the power of taking into consideration a person's community, cultural grounding, and personal history when entering a partnership. We know that there's much to lose when we make business deals in the conventional way, independent of a deeper understanding of someone's whole personhood.

Right Relationship

As I was thinking about how I wanted to open this chapter, the voice of my friend Sonya Renee Taylor landed in my heart. I am captivated by Sonya's ability to source language that pulls layers of response from me. Sonya always reminds me that transformational relationships are foundationally soul-changing experiences that reshape your belief system. Encouragement, trust, honesty, and generosity can make us feel seen, loved, connected, capable, and worthy. An award-winning poet and international best-selling author of *The Body Is Not an Apology: The Power of Radical Self-Love*, Sonya is an oracle who calls it like she sees it. I call on Sonya when I want to be precise with language, and I am excited to have her thoughts on transformation and right relationship.

Sonya and I talked over Zoom about what she thought about the possibility of a transformation happening inside finance for Black companies. It didn't take her long to get to the heart of the question:

> I think we have to start from the recognition that the foundation upon which we're moving has not been in right relationship. Oftentimes we jump into these economic dynamics or these exchange-based relationships and we assume, like, "Oh, I have really good intentions. And so that's what matters, right?" I think that what we forget is, you know, the best intention in the world does not erase impact. I could intend to make a sweet potato pie, but if I only put in turnip, then I have a turnip pie. That's what it is. Right? So the question is, what are the ingredients?

What's the foundation in which we are moving into this relationship? And can we get honest about that? Because if you can get honest about the foundation, then you can start to say, "All right, what's here that isn't serving the goal of transformation? What's here that isn't serving the goal of right relationship? Let's tell the truth about that."

Sonya grounded me in the understanding that we have to start with the foundation of being in right relationship. Right relationship is a founding value of our work at RUNWAY; we use it as a guiding framework for our capital raises and for our capital placements. Those investments are cocreated with people who also have a vision of transformation of the financial infrastructure. Together, we get to move in right relationship, which in turn makes the experience of moving money more abundant and joyful.

I first encountered the concept of right relationship through my Buddhism practice, and I have also learned from Indigenous communities and their articulation of their interconnected and interdependent relationship to all things around them. I've always sat with the concept as a very Afro-Indigenous idea that embodies the notion of *ubuntu*: I am because you are, and I move accordingly. By centering right relationship, I aspire to honor Afro-Indigenous ways of being. I agree to operate with one another in integrity and to honor our interconnectedness, by moving from the understanding that our individual well-being is connected with the well-being of others and of the earth. And the benefits of focusing on relationship in this way are not limited to increased financial output. When I focus on integrity of relationship, all the metrics of business dealings improve.

In my years of study and practice, I have learned that in order to get the transformational outcomes we want and to effect the change we need, we have to transform ourselves, our behaviors, and our systems. And being honest is the first step to creating better relationships with

Black founders. When we think about being in right relationship, we are inviting truth-telling to become a central force inside our relationships. We can begin to see that if we are not being honest by telling the truth to ourselves and others, we run the risk of repeating transactional relationship patterns.

Sonya posed the question, "Can you get honest about your intentions?" She went on to share that "a lot of times, we're like, 'I want to do Believe-in-You Money,' when it really is all about 'boost-my-self-esteem money,' or 'here's-a-way-I-can-control-and-navigate-power money.'" In addition to discussing the idea of being critical about intentions, Sonya and I spoke about how telling the truth about who we are, what we want, and the historical discrimination that's resulted in wealth inequality is important if we want to initiate and experience transformation. "So we have got to get honest, right?" she posed.

> Because what happens is, when you're not in right relationship with yourself, and you go into those dynamics, you create more harm. You actually just create more harm. And so if your commitment is not to create harm, then you'll start with saying, "Can I get honest about what underlies my actions right now?" And tell the truth about that. It doesn't mean don't invest the money, but it means you need to deal with you, too—whatever that entails. And that's not just if you are a person of racialized privilege or have a high net worth, right? We give money to our families. We invest in people in our families. And we're doing it for power; we're doing it for control; we're doing it for self worth. So, you know, get honest with yourself.

Getting honest with oneself is an important practice for anyone seeking to build more transformational relationships. By asking and answering the questions Sonya posed, we can become the change we need and ultimately transform our systems.

Truth-Telling

If being in right relationship is foundational to having a transformational relationship, then truth-telling is the anchor. For a society built on lies about its foundations—and particularly about where its wealth has come from—truth-telling is probably the most essential ingredient for transformation. During my conversation with Konda Mason (in chapter 9), a brilliant colleague, friend, and wisdom keeper, Konda shared, "When truth-telling happens, the repair can happen. Real repair can't happen if you put a Band-Aid on anything. And so when we create these relationships, we can't skip over that part." She continued: "Our financial system is so transactional that it will stay transactional if we do not tell the truth and do the real repair. I think we have to do deep work, separately and together. And then we can learn to love, then we can possibly create a system that loves Black folks. But that's what I think it's going to take. We can't skip over the hard work."

Truth-telling means getting real with yourself. If you are not willing to step into the work from a place of repair, you should not do it, because this could create more trauma and more harm. Be true to yourself by being honest about what you need, what you want, and what you expect, and also about your own limitations. The worst thing we can do is start and not complete the assignment. Black people have experienced too many people making promises that they had no intention of keeping. Transformational relationships ask for our honesty, our sincere self-reflection, and our deep exploration of the values, beliefs, attitudes, and assumptions we hold about ourselves and the world around us.

Consider the concept of so-called color blindness. "Well-meaning" White Americans have been known to claim that they "don't see color"—they just see *you*. But that is not truth-telling. Color blindness is a fallacy, and a dangerous one at that. If you commit to not seeing my Blackness, for example, you're also implicitly committing to ignoring the richness of the legacy I stand in and the relentlessness of the barriers that my ancestors and I have pushed through. When we use such terms as "underserved" or "underrepresented," we're using them as proxies without being clear about the identities of the people we're referring to. And the particulars of identity are so crucial. Without seeing the whole constellation of factors that affect someone's financial situation, we're lending through a limited lens.

Truth-telling shows us that the real need is to focus our energy on pairing our good intentions with informed and aligned actions. Truth-telling shows us that the system in which we have been operating is historically rooted in White supremacy. Asking questions about where and how the roots of this delusional and oppressive system show up inside our investing process is critical. "Let's get honest about that," Sonya said.

> Because if we can tell the truth about that, then we can say, "All right, let's control that. Let's do the best that we can to honor that, to acknowledge it, and to navigate around the dynamics that it brings up." But if we're not going to be honest about that, then we can't do anything. And so I think that the first place is, can we get honest about the nature of the relationship? That unto itself is transformational. Can we be honest about the dynamics that are present, so that we can then deal with the repercussions of those dynamics? Because until we do that, we can't build anything together.

There is no possible way to move this work forward if we are not going to be honest about the history of racism and its impact on our economic system.

Worthiness

A quick online search of the word pairing "worthiness and money" returns several pages that make clear the popularity of the topic. Though it may be a popular topic in the blogosphere, it's something that is not discussed nearly enough in the Black-owned business financing space. A lot of people, not just business owners, have experienced shame and blame and stress about money, which I unpack more in chapter 7. For now, I invite you to simply notice how sometimes those feelings can spill over into how we see ourselves, which, in turn, creates ideas that we are not good enough or that we are somehow failing. This is where money can affect our perception of our self-worth.

Self-worth is the internal belief of being good enough and worthy of love, of feeling secure to belong just as you are. Too often our money conversation gets connected to our worthiness, and it creates a false belief that we have to be more, do more, or produce more to get the resources we need. As Sonya shared with me, "Inside of this notion of right relationship is the idea of radical self-love that says we are inherently enough, that we are inherently worthy. We arrived here on this planet, imbued with worthiness. We don't have to achieve it; it can't be externally gained; it is simply who it is that we are." She also explained how we get socialized into questioning our own worthiness, saying, "Over time, the systems and structures of exploitation and extraction tell us that, in order to be enough, we need some external source. And that external source is money, that external source is power, that external source is some physical aesthetic. Those are the things that make us feel we are 'enough.'"

What makes us enough? Answering this question is at the heart of transformational relationships. In a transformed investing space, doubts about being enough and worthiness should be addressed so that they can be resolved. Having a direct intention around this matters; I have watched a lot of Black founders enter into business deals with people who are not truly values-aligned on racial equity and justice, only to endure a hellish, transactional relationship that often ended in the founder being ousted. I have also seen too many Black founders, myself included, having to navigate serious bouts of imposter syndrome. Imposter syndrome is when you doubt your talents and skills and downplay your accomplishments.

When I see Black founders in this state of mind, I quickly remember that the reflection that we sometimes see is housed in a system that has historically asserted that Black people are unworthy and not enough.

I remember listening to an interview on the NPR podcast *Planet Money* about how America determines the worth of people. The episode, "Lives vs. the Economy," aired in April 2020 and elevated a conversation about how, during the pandemic, America determined whether it should shut down the economy to save lives, or whether it should let people die to save the economy.[2] For me, this is such a wild question, but it turns out that the answer is even wilder.

The podcast describes a 1980s America with very little regulation over things that we take for granted today, like having a hazardous chemical labeled as such on a bottle. At the time, the Occupational Safety and Health Administration (OSHA) was proposing that businesses should have to label hazardous chemicals because workers had a right to know when they're working with dangerous substances. OSHA needed to understand how much it would cost to make this change and asked W. Kip Vicusi, an economist at Vanderbilt University who specializes in the economics of risk and uncertainty, for help.[3]

How does America determine worth? Up until the 1980s, it was calculated by loss of earnings due to early death. The thought was that, when someone dies early, they lose all the years of life in which they would be working and earning money. That lost future income is called the cost of death, and it has historically guided the determination of things like workers' rights, insurance policies, and how justice is accounted for in wrongful death lawsuits. That was until Vicusi challenged the underlying idea of what a life is worth by suggesting that risk is based on the risk the person was taking in doing the work. This reframe would fundamentally alter the evaluation system of risk.

As antiracist investors, we, too, have to challenge the system about who and what really matter. At the heart of it, transactional relationships only reinforce a lack of dignity. There's nothing dignified about seeing people only as vessels for the profit they can generate—or as simply sources of mass capital, in the case of high-net-worth individuals. To be doing transformational investing means that we see the worthiness of ourselves and each other, acknowledging that we all matter beyond what we produce and what capital we generate. And when we intentionally choose to relate in these deeper ways, it not only benefits the person on the receiving end but also changes the whole dynamic of how we move with each other.

How Believe-in-You Money Creates Transformational Relationships

Believe-in-You Money expands our vision and our capacity for meaningful and transformational relationships. It reminds us that being in right relationship is about understanding our inherent value, dignity, and worth, and that if we understand that we are inherently valuable and worthy, then by extension our relationships will not be extractive. In Sonya's words, "Right relationship says, 'I come to this experience from a place of dignity. And I come to this experience by recognizing your dignity. And from that place, we talk about what it is that we need, that allows both of our dignities to remain intact.'"

To get to a transformational relationship, we have to be honest with ourselves about what motivates us and about the historical impacts of racism that we are navigating. This truth-telling is so important to creating a loving economy. Additionally, both inner work and outer work are necessary if we want to change the way our current system responds to Black founders and the impact this has on them.

At RUNWAY, a part of our understanding of how we transform our relationships with Black founders is all about how we create more space for them to thrive. In our contemporary "grind culture," one is expected to be productive at all times in order to be deemed valuable or worthy. As a result, business ownership has often come to mean that one is hustling forever.

Instead of honoring these dominant attitudes, RUNWAY values a culture that encourages rest because we know that the need to stay busy is just an expression of capitalism. Our internal work culture helps us practice the transformed world we imagine by identifying and rejecting the priorities of grind culture. For example, we have an unlimited paid-time-off program and offer insurance plans for both mainstream and traditional medicine. Our goal is to repair the relationship between capitalism and Black founders by working on ourselves and doing meaningful investment work with others who are also doing their personal work.

Transformation relies on laying the groundwork for the outcomes we hope to achieve. I don't think we can achieve dynamic relationships without first imagining and then preparing for them through intentional design. By imagining and carefully laying a foundation for dynamic relationships with Black founders, we set ourselves in motion to attract that experience. The inner work of truth-telling about systems and our relationships to them, along with the ability to embrace and feel secure in our worth, can help us move toward right relationship.

Building transformational relationships is not easy, but it is worthwhile. There may be times where you want to give up, as in the story I shared about the computer system button. Other times, you may feel afraid to consider what these systems of oppression have created within our lives. For this, Sonya says, we must give ourselves grace and compassion:

> If I can start from the understanding that I didn't make myself, right? Like that's actually the only place where I think intention really matters. I didn't intend to be indoctrinated with systems that propagate marginalization and oppression; I didn't intend that. But I do have the responsibility and the accountability to undo how I was made when I realize that it harms myself and others and has given me certain dynamics and ways of thinking, and that those things don't serve me, don't serve my intention, then I can tell the truth, right? And when you can tell the truth, then it becomes so much easier to create a path towards transformation.

If there is one thing that I would caution to stay away from, it's the shame and blame that make us think we are bad people. Sonya and I—and everyone else whose voices fill the pages of this book—share the belief that shame and blame only stand in the way of the potential transformational power of lending. We believe that Black founders can have a better experience if we work to heal so that we can decenter our shame and blame and instead deepen our capacity to face and accept the truth, and then move forward accordingly. If we cannot face the truth, we cannot be resilient. Without the ability to honestly collaborate in the face of the many challenges that businesses face, shame and blame will take over in the more difficult moments. It's not enough to stop when we face barriers of the current oppressive system. We have to be able to make progress in spite of this. The exploitative capitalist system under which we live thrives on our discouragement; it relies on our lack of willingness to persist. Believe-in-You Money demands that we don't get sucked into these systemic traps.

This alternative way of relating can help Black founders move away from a paradigm of chasing grants and filling out applications only to never hear anything back, and toward something more dignified, sustainable, and joyful. We think the way to get there is through transformational relationships that are rooted in truth-telling and practices that are trusting and transparent. By setting an intention to move beyond transactional relationships and into transformational ones, we will create intergenerational equity and economic sustainability for Black communities. With transformation as a core belief, we can make Black business success the top of the political agenda and central to our personal and societal belief systems. Together, we can shift the global paradigm toward Black business sustainability and investing that is rooted in right relationship as an integral part of what it means to be in community with one another and the planet.

CHAPTER 5

Shared Risk versus Risk Averse

MONUMENT OF A CRIME[1]
Department of Justice Deserts a Fateful Building
Washington Post 25 June 1899

FAILURE OF FREEDMAN'S BANK
Big Brown-stone Building Across from the Treasury
Was Once the Depository of the Savings of Thousands
of ex-Slaves—Real Estate Speculation Ruined the
Institution, with Which Many Noted Names Were
Connected—Caused Much Distress.

Above is the opening line from an article about the former headquarters of the Freedmen's Savings Bank, the onetime depository institution chartered by the United States to assist the economic participation of newly freed Black Americans—supporting their ability to save money, their integration into an economic society, and their overall financial development. In its 10 years of existence, the Freedmen's Bank brought both hope and heartache to the Black community. Signed into law by Abraham Lincoln on March 3, 1865, only weeks before his assassination, the

Freedmen's Bank had over 70,000 depositors with more than today's equivalent of $50 million in deposits. It is almost impossible to imagine this kind of money amassed among Black Americans in the nineteenth century, but thanks to Black soldiers, families, businesses, churches, and charitable organizations, the bank thrived, with 37 offices in 16 states and the District of Columbia.

The Freedmen's Bank was led by 50 White men who served as the board of trustees. The leader of the board was Henry Cooke, brother of Jay Cooke, who was the major railroad investor who helped fund the Union war effort.[2] Many other prominent leaders of the day also sat on the board. Because it was meant for a vulnerable community, the bank's original charter did not allow for loan making, and only allowed for low-risk investments in order to "offer security, stability, and economic growth to its account holders."[3] But in 1870, after an impressive and fruitful first five years, something changed. Seeing the high volume of deposits going into the bank, the board petitioned Congress to amend the bank's charter to permit investment of the funds in real estate. This gave bank managers the legal privilege of engaging in real estate speculation. Just four years later, the bank was in financial ruin and closed for good. All of the bank's assets were liquidated, and the profits were given to the federal government. Nothing was ever returned to the newly freed Black people.

The impact of the theft of Black people's money is far-reaching and beyond measure. The history of the Freedmen's Bank and other examples of bait-and-switch tactics leveled against Black communities have led to a generational distrust of the banking system and investment strategies that persists to this day. According to the FDIC (Federal Deposit Insurance Corporation), nearly half of Black households are currently underbanked or unbanked.[4] Freedmen were encouraged to join the bank because of its emphasis on trustworthiness and congressional oversight. When depositors saw images of Frederick Douglass, who was associated with the bank, they saw this representation as a sign of promise and reputational value.

The conclusion of the 1899 *Washington Post* article quoted above shines a light on the wreckage that the freedmen who trusted the bank endured:

> Hundreds of colored men in the District of Columbia can testify to the bankruptcy of the institution. One who is now a doorkeeper in one of the departments tells the writer how he had risen to the distinction of a contractor at the time of the boom in street building of the Shepherd regime; how the failure crippled him so that he could not pay his men and how it finally resulted in his financial ruin. An ex-slaveholder tells a pathetic story of one of the trusted servants of his household who, within a few years after the war, was wearing fine clothes and boasted of the hundreds of dollars he had on deposit in the Freedmen's Bank. He had almost starved himself and his family in his effort to get rich. Every dollar was swept away, and he gave up the game and died of a broken heart. The wreck and ruin that followed the cyclone of the failure could not be described in a library full of volumes, and Congress has up to the present time refused to appropriate money to reimburse the sufferers, most of whom are now beyond the reach of pecuniary relief.[5]

The story of the Freedmen's Bank is all about risk. Who was ultimately at risk? Who can take risks? Who cannot? Who is told the truth about the risks they're taking? Who is lied to? That the leaders of the bank were not charged with a crime is horrendous and painfully unsurprising. But these men, these so-called leaders, were the type of men the systems—and the calculation of risk—were made to favor. With no real regard for the humanity of the formerly enslaved, they made decisions that placed their depositors' lives at risk. The federal government exploited the soldiers who fought for the Union, along with their families and friends, all of whom believed wholeheartedly that their deposits would be honored by the government. In *The Souls of Black Folk*, W. E. B. Du

Bois recalls the lure of the Freedmen's Bank: "With the prestige of the government back of it, and a directing board of unusual respectability and national reputation, this banking institution had made a remarkable start in the development of that thrift among Black folk which slavery had kept them from knowing."[6] History, however, has shown that the American government did not make good against the claims of the depositors or their descendants.

Redefine Risk

Power has everything to do with how risk is defined and who gets to define it. Risk is defined based on social assumptions about who the innovators and disruptors should be and on a set of ideas that support the prosperity of one group but not others. For as long as American history has been told, White men have had the privilege of "failing forward" in business. If they make a mistake, it's billed as exploration, discovery, or even a step toward greatness. When Black people or women—or anyone else who is not a White man—misstep, it comes at a cost and often leads to a setback, a demotion, a loss of funding, and so on. Many Black founders have come to believe they have to be "twice as good" in order to mitigate the risks of racism. But even then, it's not enough. At every turn of the entrepreneurial journey, racial bias appears as a roadblock. The only way to truly mitigate racism is to dismantle its hold on our systems and relationships. Black founders could be eight times as good as White founders, and that still wouldn't remedy the racism they face.

Every investment carries a possibility that the money will not be repaid, that the business will sour, or that the best-laid plans will fall apart. That's the risk of doing business. But more broadly, the question becomes, Who should bear the responsibility of the decline of the company? Assessing risk has almost always been approached through a zero-sum lens that leaves community, mutual connectivity, and more out of the equation. It's time we reevaluate the concept of risk. Believe-in-You Money and other transformational finance practices invite us to interrogate and reorganize our approaches.

In investor-speak, risk assessment determines the likelihood of loss on an asset, loan, or investment. Assessing risk helps determine how worthwhile a specific investment is and the best strategies to mitigate risk. We accept this practice without much thought. However, we know that bias is real and that it has a real, negative impact. Limiting beliefs about people or a general lack of cultural awareness will cause an underwriter to assume that there is a risk even when there isn't one.

Consider one of the most common measurements of risk: the credit score. The credit score is the bedrock of modern lending and investment and is used to assess the financial stability and creditworthiness of a person. Here's the catch, though: credit scores are based on *past* financial performance. They look back at history to make judgments about the future. We know that in America the past and present alike are filled with structural racism and biases that have shaped the ways we evaluate creditworthiness. As a result, the credit scores of wealthier and older White American homebuyers are an average of 57 points higher than those of Black homebuyers.[7] Years of discrimination in employment, lending policies, debt collection, and criminal prosecution have left Black families struggling to make ends meet and often unable to establish solid credit. People with lower credit scores find themselves on a slippery slope, often having to make decisions that negatively affect their credit scores in order to simply get by. If you're constantly trying to keep up and never able to establish a solid financial foundation, you inevitably have less ability to invest in growing a business.

In part because we understand the systemic racism embedded in credit score calculations, we don't use them in our underwriting at RUN-WAY. And neither should you. There are so many more telling, fairer, and more equitable ways to understand a business owner's ability to repay, like looking at their business model or ensuring they have proper business advising. RUNWAY uses community-based underwriting, which includes character-based lending, bringing together community members from the business space with lending professionals to determine whether a borrower's loan application is within the financial institution's policies relative to risk for extending credit.

In a conventional financing process, a founder typically submits an application, bank statements, tax returns, financial forecasts, cosigners, collateral, lease/insurance requirements, credit score, and other financial documents. Then the financial institution takes that information and puts it into an automated system that calculates a score. If the application meets a certain score, the loan officer moves forward with further due diligence to write a credit memo and share with the firm's credit committee for a lending decision. If the application does not meet a certain score, the founder may be denied right away. RUNWAY's community underwriting process is rooted in the Believe-in-You Money framework, which means we prioritize transformational relationships—not transactional ones—that invite investors to consider factors beyond a three-digit reduction of a person's wholeness.

RUNWAY relies heavily on the business education we provide to the founders we work with. We collaborate on projections and business plans to manage risk. This process creates confidence within the founder because they are realistic about repayment responsibilities. And when issues come up, we make sure we talk about them from a transparent and easy-to-navigate place. Power is also shifting in the underwriting committee; as they learn more deeply from the business education and advising side, underwriters gain a more holistic understanding of the entrepreneur and their needs, which better positions them to reduce rather than cause harm. Further, RUNWAY never asks for collateral or lien owing to the racial wealth gap and the psychological harm that entrepreneurs of color experience when they have to sign away their home or car.

Shared Risk

I wanted to talk more about risk, so I invited my friend Brendan Martin
to have a jam session with me. Brendan is the cofounder of Seed Commons, a national network of locally rooted, nonextractive loan funds that
invest in local cooperative businesses. Seed Commons doesn't use credit
scores either. It supports cooperative companies, democratic governance,
and nonextractive loans. Nonextraction for Seed Commons is defined
as ensuring that returns to the lender do not exceed the wealth that a
loan creates for the borrower.[8] "Right now," Brendan shared, "our economy is based around privileging those who have assets and making sure
they don't lose their assets. Our society governs around trying to avoid
economic risk, purely on the loss of dollars. If we wanted a society that
loves Black people, that idea would have to be gone. We would have to
stop centering pools of capital and the private ownership of capital, and
start centering people."

If we centered people as Brendan suggests—and as Believe-in-You
Money calls for—we could have a completely different experience. We
tend to talk about risk and finance as coded language that really just
means loss of wealth—and loss of wealth for a very small group of people,
at that—without any consideration for the other, very real losses that can
be incurred. My conversation with Brendan reminded me that we never
consider the thousands of people involved in the launching of a new factory. What if that factory folds? Who is at risk: the investors or the
workers? In our meaning making about risk, we are too often talking
about financial risk, focusing only on loss of assets, without considering
risk to the planet or to the people. Brendan elevated for me the ways in
which assessing risk is really about identifying what's sacred:

One unpacking of this actually involves the concepts of sacred, because
we say, "Risk is about, what can we not lose?" And dollars end up being what's sacred. The number one rule is that everything has to work

around dollars if the preservation of capital is what matters most. We can avoid bad impacts on the society, on people in the village where we're building the factory, only if it doesn't cost more, rather than people being the sacred thing. How are we gonna do this investment, if we can only do it in a way that was going to most benefit the people, even if it costs more? That would be the equation—the risk to destruction of the environment or of people.

Believe-in-You Money invites us to launch our investment strategies by honoring what the community wants and needs. With this approach, your prioritization—your establishment of what's sacred—quickly lines up with what matters to the people. This is how we get to systemic change through business investment: by reimagining risk beyond a financial scorecard. This matters for everyone, not just Black founders. There are serious implications for all people if we continue to prioritize financial risk over the risks of the people. We have to make investment decisions that protect workers and communities from risks like poor working conditions, environmental degradation, and infrastructure failure. We have to change the way we think about risk in investment in the face of new technologies, some of which can track and surveil journalists, activists, and communities of color, violating their human rights.

What we need is not less risk, but to take more risk and to extend more risk, especially to the folks who've historically been denied resources. Black companies need risk capital in order to create productive assets that can be distributed widely among people. In Brendan's words, they need "teach a person to fish" money, not "give a person a fish" money. "Risk capital is what is missing," he said. "Businesses don't get started by loans alone; they get started by collateral, or by whoever's willing to put the risk up. And Black people in this country don't have those assets," Brendan shared. "Actually, very few people have assets to start a business. So, providing risk capital, knowing you're gonna lose a portion of it, because you know that investments that work will easily pay for themselves. We all know this. That's why we give tax breaks to corporations, because we think the spillover benefits will be so great. Think of the spillover benefits; don't think about you making that money back. Do five projects and hope that one succeeds and you'll be a winner."

As a society, we are deeply concerned with preserving capital, to the point that our focus on capital is actually starving the world. The real risk, it seems, is that people with excess capital—many of whom have inherited wealth that was generated unfairly and at the expense of others—do not put their money back into the economy and let others use it to try and build something beautiful and necessary. As Brendan pointed out, "Think about what the average, you know, let's be blunt about it, White kid who goes to Silicon Valley and has a crazy idea for napkins, they get millions of dollars thrown at them. The investor community knows that only one out of 10 of the ideas will work. We should provide the same kind of venture-level support for our communities."

About America's problem with risk, W. E. B. Du Bois wrote, "No sooner had Northern armies touched Southern soil than this old question, newly guised, sprang from the earth,—What shall be done with slaves?"[9] My mind keeps going back to the formerly enslaved men and women who poured all they had into the Freedmen's Savings Bank. The archival records about the bank often describe the failed institution as having been an act of "goodwill" and having "good intentions" and the "right spirit." Those words are deeply dishonest. The truth about the bank is that it was an experiment on freedmen around indoctrination into capitalism and life as a wage earner.

When the bank folded, the government did not support the restoration of the depositors back to a state of wholeness. That was intentional too. The supporters of the bank in the federal government refused to offer aid because they did not want to dilute the lesson that capitalist investment carries a risk equivalent to its promised reward. But the truth is that these newly freed Black people would have been powerless to say no when the White wealthy élite that represented the American government brought this idea of a bank to them. Du Bois also wrote, "Then in one sad day came the crash,—all the hard-earned dollars of the freedmen disappeared; but that was the least of the loss,—all the faith in saving went too, and much of the faith in men; and that was a loss that a Nation which today sneers at Negro shiftlessness has never yet made good. Not even ten additional years of slavery could have done so much to throttle the thrift of the freedmen as the mismanagement and bankruptcy of the series of savings banks chartered by the Nation for their especial aid."[10]

Can we reimagine risk? Yes. Will it change things for Black companies? Absolutely. And it will change things for all of us; too. Believe-in-You Money is about centering those most affected by decisions made about capital—the workers, the founders, the historically marginalized communities, and the planet. When we reimagine risk, we lay the foundation to move in right relationship and create transformational experiences for everyone.

CHAPTER 6

Restorative, Mutually Beneficial versus Unequal Power Dynamics

W hen Lil' Kim said, "Money, power, respect are the keys to life," I believed her. Economically speaking, money *is* power. Money buys goods and allows us to get what we want—if we have the money. If we don't have the money, we must have access to credit to get by. Without either, the ability to protect and provide for oneself lessens, and the possibility of being exploited increases. This paves the way for power to be taken from people of lesser financial means.

We don't have enough conversations about the power dynamics of money. Those that have it wield a level of influence in the world that directs political outcomes and shapes the social destinies of strangers across the world. Throughout the course of my life, Americans have been indoctrinated in the ways of capitalism, which structures capital and power in favor of Whiteness. American history textbooks from the early 1900s explicitly drilled into students the idea that power was for Whites and Black inferiority was an absolute given, whereas contemporary books continue to emphasize these myths more implicitly. These lessons have shaped everything, including our individual and collective relationships with capital, and they have everything to do with our underinvestment in Black-owned businesses.

Whether we realize it or not, American democracy has depended on Black inequality to sustain White privilege. From bulldozing functioning Black neighborhoods and replacing them with public housing projects, to aggressive policing, mass incarceration, and community-unfriendly tax abatements, these systemic injustices have stripped access and power from Black people and their communities and, as a result, have kept inequalities alive and thriving. The construction of the highway system provides insight into this strategic and systemic stripping of power. In a *Vanderbilt Law Review* article, "White Men's Roads through Black Men's Homes," Deborah Archer writes, "Often under the guise of 'slum removal,' federal and state officials purposely targeted Black communities to make way for massive highway projects. In states around the country, highways disproportionately displaced Black households and cut the heart and soul out of thriving Black communities with the destruction of homes, churches, schools, and businesses. In some cases, entire Black communities were leveled."[1] I remember my dad, who was the mayor of the city where we lived, fighting at the state level to make sure the new interstate, I-165, would at least have on and off ramps in our community. This was 1990, and earlier plans had shown that the highway, which was meant to run directly through our Black neighborhood, would not only displace our churches, businesses, and homes but also bypass us altogether.

The highway ripping through a Black business corridor is not a metaphor for the ways Black-owned businesses are treated; the highway is a very real fact and consequence of racism in America. The highway also represents a particular choice the leaders at the time were making—to destroy rather than invest in Black companies, which in turn left them to be preyed upon in the capital market. Konda Mason, whom I mentioned earlier in the book, works at the intersection of race, land, and spirit in the American South with Black and Indigenous farmers. You'll hear more from Konda in chapter 9, but the wisdom she shares is relevant across many conversations. "I actually think that fear of knowing Black ingenuity," she says, "fear of knowing Black genius, is what prompts this system to stifle it. The people who power the system, they understand the power and potential of Black people." The strategic suppression of Black-owned businesses that's at the heart of decision making in urban planning, housing policies, and banks is rife with this impulse to stifle what Konda is talking about. "Every time you turn around," she says, "there's something to cut off our power and potential, to stop it from flowering, from thriving. I think it comes from the fear of what is possible. And so the limited opportunities are a construct to stop progress. And yet, it hasn't stopped us. It has slowed us down. There have been all kinds of obstacles in the way. But it has not stopped us." From Tulsa to Durham and beyond, Black business enclaves have over and over again been destroyed for the benefit of private wealth holders. Despite the persistent attacks on Black-owned businesses, though, the growth and innovation continue to marvel. How do we acknowledge what has happened to Black people in their pursuit of the American business dream? How do we repair the harm that has been done and create clear pathways for Black-owned businesses to grow and thrive?

No matter who I ask these questions, they say that we must start with truth-telling. Telling the truth about racism and the American economy is foundational if we hope to transform outcomes for Black-owned businesses and ultimately transform the well-being of American society. This is not easy work, but it is necessary work. Truth-telling dislodges shame and blame and gets us to act. Perhaps we fear that, in telling the truth, we will unlock so much grief and shame that we become immobilized. If the grief comes, we've got to let it come in order to heal through it.

Power, Healing, and Community

In the summer of George Floyd's murder, I was led to study African rituals of grief. Grief was my truth. And I needed my grief to be witnessed.

I was convinced that outcries in response to the theft of Floyd's life were missing an important element of the grieving process that could be a linchpin in repairing our trauma and our financial system. I began to think that if we could give ourselves permission to feel the weight of the losses we have faced because of racism and wealth hoarding, we might be able to change our course of action. Malidoma Patrice Somé, author of *Ritual: Power, Healing and Community*, talks about grieving as essential to community life and grief as a source of power. He writes, "People who do not know how to weep together are people who cannot laugh together. People who know not the power of shedding their tears together are like a time bomb, dangerous to themselves and the world around them."[2] In the absence of coming together with intention, we face the threat of unhealed wounds, piled-up traumas, and the inability to heal ourselves and our communities.

Similar to the ideas that Somé shares on communal grief, restorative justice is a practice that helps us tap into the power of community and ritual in order to set the truth free. Restorative justice is a practice for addressing harm that honors Afro-Indigenous values of reparation, inclusion, and balance. At its core, it's a ritual practice meant to bind us more deeply to one another and to our humanity. I find restorative justice compelling because it provides a framework for thinking about how to heal and restore a balance of power. Dr. Fania Davis—civil rights attorney, founder of Restorative Justice for Oakland Youth, and sister to Angela Davis, an American activist and scholar—is one of the restorative justice leaders I follow. Fania has described restorative justice as follows:

A justice that seeks not to punish, but to heal.

A justice that is not about getting even, but about getting well.

A justice that seeks to transform broken lives, relationships, and
    communities rather than damage them further.

A justice that seeks reconciliation rather than a deepening of
    conflict.

A justice that seeks to make right the wrong rather than adding
to the original wrong.
A healing justice rather than punishing justice. A restorative
justice rather than retributive justice.[3]

Restorative justice has been practiced for decades by criminal justice reform advocates and social workers, and even inside of schools—anywhere that we make human connections. The practice is less about conventional ideas of "justice" and more about centering those who have been harmed while acknowledging the humanity of those who have caused harm. Restorative justice creates space for those who've experienced harm to tell their stories, allows others to acknowledge the story as listeners and witnesses, affirms the wronged parties, and establishes plans for apologetic actions and other steps that will put things right.

In a Believe-in-You Money context, restorative justice is a process for corporations, families, and governments to tell the truth about their relationships to the racial wealth gap—and particularly to be honest about unearned financial privilege at the cost of so many others. Power dynamics can change when we talk about how different groups of people do not have the same access to resources, and how the parties that control those resources have wielded their positional power to cause harm.

When I reflect on Dr. Davis's words about transforming broken lives, relationships, and communities, I find that they deeply resonate with the concept of Believe-in-You Money. With Believe-in-You Money, we transform lives, relationships, and communities. We choose to center community, to use nonextractive capital and patient terms, and to be intentional about using an antiracist lens because we are clear that denying folks financial access is an issue of power. To remedy this embedded challenge, we have to attend to the redistribution of power. It's worth mentioning that power dynamics exist everywhere, even inside the restorative justice framework. But what I think is important to draw from the wisdom of restorative justice is the centering of relationships, the call for accountability, and the commitment to repair.

Relationships That Build Power

This chapter focuses on creating investment relationships that build power. We know that the usual dynamics of race, gender, age, sexual orientation, and socioeconomic status are creating barriers for entry. Now let's talk about how we change that. We have to create mutually beneficial and restorative conditions. Remember that restoring something is all about bringing focused attention to the well-being of that thing. We do that by being transparent about the investing process, removing unnecessary gatekeepers, and eliminating practices that contribute to inequitable access. Getting to a more restorative investment experience takes an internal approach of healing our personal money relationships, and it takes an interpersonal approach whereby in our working relationships we get real about the state and impact of power, who has it, and who does not.

Believe-in-You Money can offer guidance that helps us assess our investing relative to power dynamics. One of my colleagues who directs investments for a large fund shared a time when she was close to providing a loan, but the idea of the business being run by the worker-owners was shaking her confidence in moving forward. She talked about risk being the issue, saying, "I know that each person really wants to make this work, and that they've been organizing and educating themselves on what this capital means, but I just was uncomfortable." Despite what she shared, I didn't think it was about risk; I thought it was about power. So, I asked more questions. After giving it more thought, she added, "I know this is what the community wants and I value what the community is saying it needs, but I don't know how to work with that."

Working with money always brings power into the conversation, even when we intend to create a more liberated exchange. You can use

Believe-in-You Money as a check-in for yourself. As you open up to these ideas, take note of what is coming up. If discomfort is present, ask yourself, What's really underneath the uncomfortable feelings? I reminded my friend that Believe-in-You Money is about building power by *believing in* the communities on the receiving end of capital. The racial wealth gap, racial inequity, racial injustice—whatever language you prefer to use, it's all ultimately about power. I reminded her that in those moments of discomfort, we shift power by coming back to the basics of having transformational relationships. I proposed that she tackle this directly by being transparent with the people involved, if she was open to it. My friend quickly picked up on what I was saying, acknowledging that these exchanges should not repurpose inequity by her centering her own power and privilege. She knew that what was really needed was to reorient around the importance of following the lead and the stated needs of the people on the receiving end of her investments. This moment elevated the point that, most often, listening to the people who we intend to help in transparent and open conversation can support the understanding of this type of problematic approach.

For repair to be meaningful, we need to center those who have been harmed, and create equitable opportunities and power dynamics by pushing for more ownership and political influence. When you operate from a Believe-in-You Money place, values of power sharing, ownership, choice, and voice are used to create a more mutually beneficial process. When I think of who is getting this right in the lending space, I think of the Boston Ujima Project. According to its website, "Everyone has a voice. People work together to take care of each other. And communities have the final say over the development that impacts their streets and their families." The Boston Ujima Project is a community-driven fund that invests in locally owned businesses run by communities of color. *Ujima* means "collective work and responsibility" in Swahili. With a governing body of members voting on which businesses and resources they want to see in their communities, as well as which businesses to invest in, the Boston Ujima Project embodies its name. Members are every-day people—workers, small-business owners, activists, and investors—working together using a "democratic investment vehicle raising capital to finance small businesses, real estate, and infrastructure projects."[4]

The work of the Boston Ujima Project is Believe-in-You Money in action. Again, the central aim of this type of capital is to build power with community members by putting the power into the hands of the people to make decisions about what kinds of companies they want in their neighborhoods.

A History with Power

When my folks visit my home state of Alabama, I take them on a pilgrimage around the state to understand how Black wealth extraction and power have built America. It's like taking an economic history trip, but make it Black. Alabama possesses a history that crisscrosses racial prejudice and an economic and political power agenda that is still shaping the fate of our country today. I'll do my best to re-create the experience in writing.

Although the subject matter is dense, my Alabama pilgrimage is centered on liberation, racial healing, sacred uses of money, imagination, and joy. I am intentional about going to places that illuminate the intersections of power, money, shame, and grief because that is where the most powerful lessons can be learned. Once I'm on the land of my ancestors, I activate rituals that help provide an understanding of what repair and restoration can achieve. I pray to open my mind and my heart in order to imagine beyond our current economic reality. From that place, I start to identify, to celebrate, and to imagine new opportunities to make systemic change.

Starting in my hometown of Prichard, Alabama, inside the Africa-town region, I go to the edge of the water, where our ancestors first touched this foreign land. This is a sacred place. If you were there with me, I would ask you to think of sacred places that you have seen or maybe heard about. What are the things that let you know it was sacred? Maybe it was the stained glass, or perhaps it was the quietness and serenity. If you were with me, I would ask you to notice Africatown. Does the place feel and look like a sacred place? If you ever visit Africatown, you will learn that the edge of the water bumps up to a paper plant that dumped toxic ash on the community for over 70 years.

This is about power.

Africatown is an American story like no other, growing from the lives of 110 enslaved men and women. Brought to the United States illegally in 1860, well after the international slave trade had been abolished, they were taken as captives from Africa, enduring the horrors of the transatlantic voyage, the American Civil War, and plantation slavery before eventually establishing the settlement known as Africatown. Sylviane Diouf, author of the award-winning *Dreams of Africa in Alabama*, notes that Africatown was "the first [town] continuously controlled by Blacks, the only one run by Africans."[5] When legendary author, researcher, and filmmaker Zora Neale Hurston came to Africatown, she was looking to speak to the last survivor of the Middle Passage, Kossola, who knew firsthand what it meant to endure slavery. Kossola, also known as Cudjoe Lewis, recounted the details that ultimately became the core content of Hurston's powerful and essential book *Barracoon: The Story of the Last "Black Cargo."* Today, the descendants and the community members of Africatown produce tours, educational seminars, and stage plays as a way of both remembering and registering the truth of what happened and continues to happen to the people of this community.

Even as Africatown invites an international conversation about reparations and the restoration of people and land and well-being, the reality is that the people are not well. Africatown descendants and residents of Africatown are involved in a lawsuit against the nearby paper company for the cancer-causing pollution it has leveled on the community. For decades, thick storms of cancer-causing ash have fallen on Africatown.

Residents recall how even just a quick dash from the house to the car was enough to cause exposure. Even the measures people took, like washing their garden vegetables thoroughly and not leaving their clothes outside on the drying line for too long, couldn't protect them from the contamination. In 2020, 160 years after their ancestors defied the odds and founded their own self-reliant community after being kidnapped from Africa, the people of Africatown sued International Paper for releasing hazardous chemicals into the air and local environment.

This is about power.

Despite the health disparities, the economic exclusion, and the full-out theft of human life, Africatown continues to lift its voice, reflecting the resounding power of its ancestral legacy. Africatown will not be silenced. In Africatown, the relationship between colonization and the slave trade and the power and wealth they created is still palpable today. With a Believe-in-You Money lens, what action might be truly reparative in this context? Whatever the action, it's important that it starts with speaking the truth about the impact on Black families and the violence it has caused our global community. Perhaps if we commit to make a difference by investing Believe-in-You Money into communities like Africatown, we can begin to repair the wrongs and restore our relationships to establish more harmony among and between our communities.

Unequal Power for Black Business Owners

After leaving Africatown, I would take you to the Equal Justice Initiative (EJI) in Montgomery. One of the many reasons EJI is important is because it brings us face-to-face with the role that business and capital have played in racialized terror. Inside the Legacy Museum, intentionally located on Commerce Street—where enslaved Africans were sold and transported all around the country—we learn details of the law firms and banks in the region that profited from slavery. Many of these family names, including the infamous Lehmans, are still wealthy, active, and influential in the community today. However, it is the story of Elmore Bolling that provides a stark contrast to the story of such families.

Bolling, whose name is included in the EJI memorial, was a successful Black businessman in Alabama, working in the trucking business and as the owner of a gas station in Lowndes County, just outside of Montgomery. He was murdered in 1949 by a White neighbor, simply because he was making "too much" money.[6] The NAACP field notes said that the cause of death was being "too successful to be a Negro."[7] Not only was Bolling making more money than most, but he was also paying more money than area employers and creating pathways for other Black men who owned trucks to do deliveries. When rumors started circulating that a mob wanted him killed, Bolling made it known that he was not going to be run off for making an honest living. Later that week, he was murdered with a shot to the back; he was only 39 years old.

And while Bolling's very premature and unjust death is a massive and tragic loss in itself, the impact of his murder created irreversible waves in his family and community as well. Everyone who worked for him lost their livelihoods. All of his children dropped out of school to work in order to support their family, while their mother worked cleaning clothes. Callously opportunistic White folks insisted that the family pay supposed debts owed by their murdered patriarch. This was nothing more than a meritless shakedown, but the family was helpless in the relentlessly anti-Black environment.

The fate that Bolling met because of his success haunts me. Truth be told, the fear of this kind of response still suffocates Black people's business ambitions today. Black people imagine that if they grow too big, someone will come and take their earnings, and maybe even their life. I am clear that the violence that ended Bolling's life was meant to interrupt his ability to generate capital that racist White people perceived to be their birthright, to seize control of Bolling's wealth, and to intimidate and discourage other Black folks from following Bolling's ambitious lead. The witnesses to Bolling's murder said that the killers didn't even bother to cover their faces because they knew that nothing would happen.

This is about power.

If you have no capital, no credit, and no wealth holders or institutions to believe in you, the stage is set for a power grab. The Jim Crow era in America, during which it was commonplace for a White saboteur to murder a Black business owner for any reason they might please, is still felt today. The ill-gotten gains from Jim Crow and across American history have altered the power dynamics and economic experiences of Black people in America. The power stolen from us serves as the foundation for the way Black neighborhoods are built up (or not), how our businesses are supported and capitalized, how we access education, food, health, and more.

When we read about inhumane circumstances like the water crises in Flint, Michigan, and Jackson, Mississippi, most of us know that if those communities were majority White, safe water conditions would be a given. We know this because we understand that with power comes capital investment. And we know this because of history. The inherited legacy of racial zoning, segregation, and redlining has material consequences for Black founders' ability to build wealth. Brendan Martin, whose voice we hear in chapter 5, offered the following:

> People who are less powerful often are more extracted from, and when you get to the United States of America, and the way that the Black populations of our country have been treated since slavery and now, that exact same history of extraction tracks with the ways in which power has been used against Black populations and Brown populations. The more or less power you've had in our society, the more you've been extracted from, and often at the hands of capital. So reversing that relationship with capital is the first step towards changing the relationship people—and in our country, Black people—have with the rest of the economy and society.

Using capital to shift the power imbalance is what Believe-in-You Money is about. But to make the shift, we also have to tell the truth and do our personal change work. Here's the thing: if you know that a group of people have been traumatized, you should not retraumatize them. Black founders are in active trauma. To avoid further harming people we desire to support, each of us working with Black founders needs to understand the history of Black entrepreneurship and wealth building as a prerequisite to being in active relationship with Black businesses. The history of doing business as a Black person in America is deeper and more nuanced than can be described. Investors tend to assume that Black people start businesses only to make more money, without understanding the many other systemic barriers that motivate them to create their own circumstances. Your job as an antiracist investor is to understand the why.

Power Redistribution

Power and wealth redistribution—which is the ultimate goal of Believe-in-You Money—is how we bring economic well-being to Black communities and the businesses that anchor them. This type of redistribution redresses the uneven and unjust benefits of economic gains built on racial and ethnic subjugation, replacing them with shared power, codeveloped terms of investment, deep partnership, and, most importantly, redistributed wealth and power. Power redistribution tells us that divesting from mainstream investing isn't enough, particularly when one turns around and reinvests in a renewable energy company owned by a rich White man without considering the many other demographics of business owners who might need that investment more. When we take power into account, we see that, in order to get to a mutual benefit, we have to invest in ways that embody political values of wealth redistribution and anti-exploitation.

If you ask me how to invest with power redistribution in mind, I will point you to Nwamaka Agbo, a friend and collaborator who applied her Restorative Economics framework to support donors and investors in making values-aligned investments into disinvested and disenfran- chised communities. Nwamaka's Restorative Economics framework was born out of her social justice movement work and informed by her study of transformative justice practices and reparations frameworks. About her work with the Kataly Foundation, Nwamaka says, "We sup- port community-owned, community-governed projects that are rooted in building the political, economic, and cultural power of Black, Indige- nous and all communities of color, so that we can have self-determination, sovereignty, and we can have sacred safe space to heal."

As the founding CEO of Kataly, Nwamaka leads her team as they invest in strategies that create shared prosperity and self-determination for a just transition to the next economy. One manifestation of Kataly's work is the Restorative Economies Fund, which seeks to close the racial wealth gap and transform our financial system by strategically reinvest- ing resources into community-owned and community-governed projects led by Black people, Indigenous people, and all people of color.[8] Nwa- maka shares how her background working in social justice, policy, elec- toral organizing, and community organizing showed her that "when we're trying to organize Black and Brown people to exercise their power, there's this invisible role that money is playing, and because we haven't had access to the capital or the resources before, it's not necessarily evi- dent how the stealth influence of capital is tilting the scales away from communities in need." She points to all the ways in which a lack of transparency in financing wreaks havoc on Black people's ability to ac- cess and mobilize capital, and how she created the restorative economies framework to support people's "ability to actually understand what is the role that money can play in helping us to get free and helping us to be liberated people."

The framework gave Nwamaka a concrete tool for consistently push- ing back against the ways conventional economic development tries to appease Black and Brown people with social benefits, programs, and services, but none of the financial benefits of the development. It's one thing to promise a community a certain number of jobs or improvements to the infrastructure, but it's a different thing to allow them to own and determine their own systems. Without ownership, you don't have the control or authority to make the decisions about the systems that shape your life and are left unable to economically benefit from them. Restorative economics supports projects that create meaningful employment, resist gentrification, and increase democratic participation so that Black and Brown people benefit financially. Power dynamics can only begin to shift toward a restorative economy when we invest in the type of work Nwamaka is doing and the work of Believe-in-You Money.

When Aaron Tanaka, founder of the Center for Economic Democracy, created a powerful reimagining of traditional portfolio investing theory called Social Movement Investing (SMI), it was to help investors look at their strategies from a power lens. Aaron's theory was the topic of hours of conversation we shared about ideas for investment that restores and encourages political power. SMI is based on the idea that those closest to the pain are the best candidates to be closest to the power. Investors who practice SMI do so because they believe that deep, sustainable change can only occur when oppressed communities themselves can design, own, and govern the systemic solutions to their problems.

Drawing on frameworks from both social justice organizing and impact investing fields, SMI proposes movement-aligned capital strategies that help build the power necessary to address our many challenges, from economic and racial injustices to climate and migration crises. We cannot "impact invest" ourselves into structural and transformational change. The hope is that SMI can offer guidance on how to invest capital in alignment with social movements to amplify, augment, and strengthen power building in order to build a just, equitable, and sustainable future. Leaning into guidance like SMI or Believe-in-You Money will not change everything overnight, but it will provide us with a road map for doing our part to initiate transformational change.

Believe-in-You Money is about power—not just money power but the power of creativity, storytelling, sacredness, and agency and governance. With a commitment to redistribution of power, Believe-in-You Money can be a transformational tool as we source our deals and think about the ways power building is an important metric in regenerative capital.

CHAPTER 7

Releasing Shame and Fear versus Maintaining Secrecy and Complexity

Over the years, I've had the opportunity to hold space with some incredible people who've been willing to share their money stories with me. Something that I find striking is that everyone I speak with—successful entrepreneurs, entertainers, and athletes included—has a money story. We all have at least one defining moment that shapes the stories we tell ourselves about money and drives our behavior, assumptions, and beliefs.

After listening to many money stories, I've learned that holding on to the wrong money story can lead to keeping money secrets. Money secrets are nothing new, and our secrecy is often simply a response to what we learned as young people. But despite their innocent origins, money secrets can be harmful. Maybe we heard messages that gave us reason to believe it's typical practice to hide our money habits from the people closest to us—for example, "Don't tell your father I bought this" or "It didn't cost that much" (when in fact it did). While we may not fully understand why we do it, or even be conscious of the fact that we do, we have developed a sophisticated set of behaviors and scripts that help us keep our money secrets just that: secret.

Money Secrets

Keeping a money secret can feel harmless. People don't need to know how much you have, right? Whether you are scraping by or your money is overflowing, you can choose to keep your story to yourself. At the heart of it, I don't think financial secrecy is meant to create harm; maybe we do it to protect ourselves. Talking about money can be difficult, so we avoid the conversations altogether. But trust me when I say that keeping significant financial decisions and losses from your family can be catastrophic. Our inability to talk openly about money puts people at risk—just as it did my friend Dee.

The first time I met Dee, it was over lunch. Dee and her cofounder, Empress, were leading an incredible brand that was working to better the community. I was excited to be meeting like-minded people, and we became fast friends. Dee is one of those people who you feel like you've known your whole life, even though you've known them only a short time.

Early on I started to notice that Dee was acting differently. She was missing meetings and her work was hit or miss—sometimes she produced good work and sometimes it was not so good. I was pretty sure that something was wrong, so I asked her what was up. She blew it off by saying a family health issue was distracting her and requiring more of her time. I let it go, but I shouldn't have. Dee's behavior grew more inconsistent and concerning.

The next time I asked about what was happening, she completely shut down, telling me that for the sake of her mental health, she couldn't talk about it. One week later, Dee was dead. She had taken her own life. I later learned that the federal government filed an indictment against her for fraudulent misuse of PPP loans. You may remember that PPP, the Paycheck Protection Program, was designed to provide business owners with quick access to loans from the Small Business Administration to help with payroll and operating costs related to disruptions caused by the COVID-19 pandemic.

Overcome with shame, Dee didn't get an attorney. She didn't respond to the notices for information. She didn't ask for help.

She kept her money secret.

I am heartbroken. Dee's inability to go on living feels particularly cruel when I think about the billions of dollars in PPP loans that were forgiven. Money shame and fear are not uncommon; you can get past that moment. If you are experiencing these emotions, please call a mental health professional for help or talk to someone you trust.

Financial Stress

Both the Centers for Disease Control and Prevention and the National Institutes of Health have studies showing the correlation between debt and depression and stress. Insights from a national health poll revealed that people who reported high debt stress were more likely to have health issues such as ulcers or digestive tract issues compared with people who reported low debt stress. Similarly, 44 percent of those with high debt stress had migraines or headaches compared with 15 percent of those with low debt stress.[1]

If you are Black or a person of color, the impact of financial stress can be even more damaging. According to the report "Race, Depression and Financial Stress" by Shervin Assari, Black Americans experience higher financial distress than White Americans.[2] Owing to generational impacts of discrimination, Black households have fewer resources like savings and family help to draw on when under financial pressure. Even when Black Americans have the same income and education as White Americans, they still have much less wealth overall.[3] Specifically, data shows Black Americans are not confident about their ability to manage an emergency expense of $2,000 within a month's timeframe let alone save and plan for retirement.[4] Trouble paying bills is one of the ways that riskiness gets assigned to a person, which leads to higher interest rates and predatory deal terms.

It's important for me to say that this is *not* a personal financial problem that financial literacy can fix; this is a systemic problem. Maybe you have noticed that, over the years, companies have moved to using the courts to collect on small consumer debts, giving them power—granted by a court judgment—to garnish wages and empty the bank accounts of low-wage workers.[5]

ProPublica, an investigative newsroom, attempted to measure, for the first time, the prevalence of judgments stemming from these types of lawsuits. It found a clear pattern emerging: they were concentrated in Black neighborhoods.[6] The ProPublica article tells the story of how a single mother fell behind on her sewer bill after losing her job. The utility company filed suit and won a judgment that seized a total of $382 from her credit union account—not enough to pay the full bill, but significant in that it left her with nothing. This is how racial bias by lenders or collectors merges with generations of discrimination, making it so that Black families have nowhere to go when they come under financial pressure.

Dee felt like she had nowhere to go. I think about her all the time. I am still working to release my own shame of noticing a problem and not doing more to help. I yearn deeply for the rituals that help us heal from this kind of devastation. I have been taking my grief and my shame to the water, letting the saltiness of the ocean mix with the salt in my tears. I scream into the crashing waves and let the ocean drown out my voice, until I have given it all back to the land, the water, the air, the earth. This releasing ritual helps me invite imagination and wonder back into my spirit.

The Secret Costs of Starting Up While Black

What do grief, trauma, and shame have to do with money? Everything. The way we talk about money and the way we think about money are driven by our past experiences with money. I ask myself, How do we stop what happened to Dee from happening again?

If we want to change the system, we have to change how we engage with the stories we hold about money. The willingness to reflect on the implicit and explicit money lessons you learned as a young person and how they continue to shape your assumptions can be powerful. When I hold space for someone in these types of conversations, I often ask them to tell me about their history with money. I ask them to tell me about when they were young. What were some of the messages they learned from their parents about money? What were their attitudes toward money? Suddenly, a door opens to unlock feelings about a subject that often feels too heavy or taboo to discuss.

Black founders spend a lot of money just to learn about money. They often shell out thousands on seminars, coaches, conferences, consultants, and more to get the information they need about money to finance their companies, but these self-funded investments still don't promise them access to the opportunities and support they need. An investment fund led by Melissa Bradley, called 1863 Ventures, collects data on the current entrepreneurship playing field. Through their research, they found that Black entrepreneurs paid $250,000 more than White founders who were just starting out.[7] That figure encompasses the cost of higher interest rates, which is a result of perceived risk, leading Black founders to pay 3–13 percent more in expenses. Many Black founders also turn to consultants to help bridge the relationship and information gap. As a result, Black founders are seven times more likely to hire consultants than White founders, adding to their costs.[8]

There has always been a shroud of secrecy around how to capitalize a business. This secrecy limits who can move their ideas forward, and in particular, it excludes Black business owners from the conversation. The smaller number of Black-owned companies that get capitalization are not insignificant; in fact, we are proud of each one of those founders. But the success of the few founders who receive the capital needed does not create a trickle-down economic impact that creates change in Black communities. If we want to show real economic love to Black-owned businesses, we have to shift from the existing dominant, extractive system—a system that reinforces secrecy and overly complex processes and creates feelings of shame and guilt—to one that promotes transparency and right relationship.

The question is, Can we deal with one another in a way that is kind and equitable?

Believe-in-You Money allows Black business owners *and* those who invest in Black business owners to clearly see the path to success. It invites a holistic relationship between investors and lenders to show up as human beings, full of complexity, rich with stories and experiences that are far more expansive than the limiting stories we too often hear, tell, and reinforce about money holders. We know that secrecy and shame continue to complicate the pathway of getting and giving money, and that they affect both entrepreneurs and capital holders alike. Transformation is possible if we choose transparency and lean into truth-telling, vulnerability, and compassion.

The bottom line is that Black entrepreneurs need the type of financial support that comes from people who have done the internal work that helps them release their own shame and guilt around money. When non-Black people—particularly White people and others who've internalized Whiteness—haven't done this work but want to "support" Black-owned businesses, their shame and guilt limit their beliefs, and the impacts of these limitations then land on the founders and employees of Black-owned companies. I remember speaking with a potential investor for our fund who asked me, "Do Black entrepreneurs really need the money?" I was kind of in shock, and I asked him what he meant.

But I knew what he meant. He had been wrongly led to believe that plentiful capital was available but that Black people were simply not applying. That sometimes founders seek out investment but the business simply does not meet the fund's criteria. That everything is fair and equitable. He did not understand that having access to capital and having capital that is accessible are two very different things. He was responding from a place that acknowledges neither the privileges he experiences that limit his perspective nor the barriers to access that Black founders face.

The Believe-in-You Money framework asks us to challenge our limiting beliefs. Maybe we think there is no way that we can change our financial practices. Believe-in-You Money invites us to challenge ourselves, to ask ourselves why we think the status quo economic reality can't be changed. Or what could be possible if it *were*. Or remember that there were different economic realities before the one we live in now, and people of the past likely couldn't imagine the economy of the present. When we reflect critically in these ways, we realize that underneath the beliefs that drive our behaviors is a story that we have been telling ourselves for years. It's time to understand that story. It's time to believe something else is possible.

Releasing Shame

My friend Anu Gupta, a talented attorney and mindfulness and yoga leader, is the founder of Be More with Anu, a company that trains organizations in breaking bias. I asked Anu what insights from his work he could share with me about letting go of shame and guilt. No surprise, our conversation quickly turned to how the stories we tell can either limit or accelerate real change.

Anu works with what he calls early adopters—lawyers, doctors, bankers, and engineers at different companies who want to transform their thoughts and behaviors to be aligned with their intentions. Early adopters understand that, in order to undergo this transformation, they have to confront the shame and guilt they feel about the story of Whiteness and money. According to Anu, "This is the place where we're all connected." He points out that Whiteness limits White people and that eliminating anti-Blackness from our systems is good for all of us. "Because when an economy loves Black people," he says, "actually all White people will be liberated from this made-up story of Whiteness."

But as Anu can tell you, moving us from our current shameful relationship with money and race into a paradigm of a transparent economy that loves Black people is not easy. "Shame," he shares, "is one of those afflictive emotions that prevents behavior change. If we continue to marinate in shame, we are basically going to disengage; we're going to feel debilitated; and we're not going to take action. So in order to confront this truth, if shame comes up, we welcome it. But we have to transform it."

Transforming money shame is a responsibility we all must carry. As a society, we are constantly told to pursue more. More money, more success, more things—just *more*. We have been told that hyperproductivity will make us happier and leave us feeling more fulfilled. In contrast to this claim, I meet so many entrepreneurs who are feeling burned out. They don't have to tell me why; I know the reasons why. The dominance of capitalism and its relentless privileging of Whiteness are exhausting. This is true not only for Black people but also for non-Black people who are tired of holding up a financial system that was designed for the kind of exploitation and political disempowerment that goes along with a racial caste system. To this point, Anu says,

> The current capitalism paradigm is that we aren't taught very much about money in our school systems. In our society, we talk more about sex than money. We talk more about everything else. But money, even though we're this hypercapitalist society, people are just not trained in the basics of what money is, how it grows, what it's supposed to do. And that is a huge barrier for a lot of people—particularly for a lot of Black and Brown people—to enter the market. So we're constantly hustling; we're constantly taught the scarcity mentality. And that is just a paradigm shift. To really not think of money as something external,

but something that's internal, that you attract. And for that, I think we really have to release shame first. And then guilt is going to arise because probably each one of us has made a lot of bad decisions around money, ourselves, or others. I know I have, and I sometimes do. But the exciting thing is, all those decisions are in the past. And we still have the present and the future.

The scarcity mentality that Anu points to encourages and rewards—and in some cases demands—constant hustling. As we encounter relentless conditioning that emphasizes maximizing profit in the absence of grounding guidelines or values, we can find ourselves spinning around trying to chase it, without attending to our own needs and well-being, or even to the impact that we truly want to create.

The way Anu describes money in terms of energy, on the other hand, puts the onus on the individual to get clear about one's relationship to money—to center one's self and go from there. Too often the question we pose is, How can I do more to get more money? rather than, How do I attract money and make it do more for me?

Confronting and transforming our limiting beliefs by releasing shame is the work that needs to be done. When I asked Konda Mason about how to release shame, she recommended that we "go backwards. Learn about your family." "Learn about where your wealth has really come from. Learn. Go back, go back, go back." "I think," she said, "when you start healing the places in your past regarding wealth, you heal your psyche."

By looking into the money story, we can transform our attitudes and beliefs—a transformation that we all must undergo if we hope to experience an economy that loves Black people. The system is currently set up to count us out when we face challenges rather than to support our recovery from such challenges. And since the system is neither color-blind nor class-blind, it disproportionately counts out the people who end up needing the most support as a result of the systemic barriers and discrimination they face.

Believe-in-You Money invites us to go in the other direction. Let's throw the credit score out the window and instead prioritize more understanding, patient, and gracious metrics to gauge investments. When we bring curiosity to the stories we hold, we allow space for the truth to reveal itself and for past harms to be repaired. As we release shame and guilt, we can explore more honest, courageous, and liberatory ideas about money.

Money is a taboo subject for many people, and my hope is that this book helps us make space to talk about it. Even though it affects our lives in so many ways, there is an unspoken rule that we shouldn't talk about money. Whether we have too little, just enough, or an overflow, we are all connected to the subject. In the absence of open conversations about money, the people who really need the systems to change are less likely to get the support they need because we allow our discomfort and fear to immobilize us. In the current paradigm, we leave too much space for misunderstanding to build, for anxiety and stress to increase, and for promising ventures and important relationships to deteriorate. We keep our cards close to our chest, which means we miss out on connecting with the people around us and ultimately cut off the many opportunities available to us through those people and potential relationships.

When we humanize the process of lending and borrowing capital, we create more possibility for deeper meaning making with one another. How can we transform our relationship to money so that we think of it as an enabler, while also leveling the field in terms of whose dreams it enables? What I imagine on the other side of this transformation is the depth and richness of all that truly is available.

CHAPTER 8

Collective Action versus Go It Alone

In case the structure and spirit of this book haven't already made this clear, everything I know about investing I learned from my community. When my dad ran for mayor, the community held fish frys to raise money for the campaign. This was their way of investing in a vision they could get behind. When my mom was battling cancer, my community invested in her and in me. They cooked meals for Mom, took her to doctors' appointments, and advocated for her health when she could not. When Mom passed away, folks in the community made sure I knew that, just as much as I was hers, I was theirs too and would never be alone.

I was raised by strong Black women and good Black men who invested in themselves. They were educated and traveled, with notable senses of fashion and deep appreciation for art. And they made sure they nourished me: I ate food made with love and inherited a nourishing diet of global music and rituals that sustain me to this day. My first investments came from community members in the Black church. This community made sure I knew how to speak up for myself and taught me to be principled, to stand up for justice and goodness. Just before I went away to college, the women at church, from their white-church-glove-adorned hands, gave me a white envelope stuffed with cash, for the "little extras" I would need while away from home.

I wanted to return to my church roots to ground this chapter because so much of what I learned about the power of community and collective action came from my early church life. There, I was introduced to a movement of people committed not only to the enrichment of our personal lives but also to the holistic well-being of Black people. This investment in mutual care—the seed that ultimately grew into my commitment to Black folks' financial and overall well-being—was evidence of what we call the beloved community.

American philosopher Josiah Royce is credited with coining the term in 1913, but the Reverend Dr. Martin Luther King Jr. brought it back into public view in the late 1950s. Centered on the economic and social inclusion of all people, beloved community is about collective action. It's about building up a critical mass of people committed to and trained in the philosophy and methods of nonviolence so that they can *act* together to end racism, militarism, and poverty. Starting with the beloved community as my grounding for this chapter helps me explain how I came to understand—from a moral and spiritual place—the importance of coming together for justice.

I was excited to talk about the concept of beloved community with Pastor Andrew Wilkes, who cofounded the Double Love Experience Church in Brooklyn, NYC, with his wife, Pastor Gabby. Pastor Andrew explains, "Beloved community is a conviction that we are not just interacting with one another as disconnected and distant, atomized individuals, but that there's an underlying unity and point of solidarity that fits us together." Beloved community honors and reinforces the threads that weave our individual lives into a shared experience.

Believe-in-You Money is grounded in the belief in beloved community. Like Believe-in-You Money, beloved community asks us to come together to act—not just for ourselves but for one another—in order to end racial injustice and wealth inequality. Pastor Andrew talks about the ways that his biblical grounding of beloved community intersects with the thinking of Believe-in-You Money. "In order to align where you place your dollars with where your heart is, Jesus says, 'Where your treasure is, there your heart should be.' And if we place capital, place tithes and offerings, checks, coins, Cash Apps right where racial justice is, where undoing White supremacy is, then it shifts the lens that we bring to the world we inhabit." Pastor Andrew's words are a powerful reminder that by financially resourcing efforts that have been systemically denied access, we can radically shift the power dynamic in our society and undo injustice. That is belief in action. Believe-in-You Money becomes the experience of what's possible when inequities are addressed and long-held and inaccurate misconceptions that thrive in a society with a scarcity mind-set are transformed.

After our conversation spanned many topics and perspectives, Pastor Andrew brought it full circle, adding his thoughts about how beloved community supports Black founders and their businesses beyond just writing a check. "The well-being of Black folks," he says, "is not just about, you know, some impersonal meeting ground of buyers and sellers trying to exchange what goods and services they have, but rather: Can we meet all of our people's needs? Can we match our talents and our gifts to folks' deepest aspirations in ways that are nonextractive and nonexploitative, and that really provide an opportunity for folks' deep creativity to be facilitated?"

What Pastor Andrew is calling for is an investment that goes beyond goodwill and brings a deep commitment to the whole person and community as an outcome of success. The depth of investing we are calling for is not common. I do believe that if we are going to see investment as a tool for change, we will have to change ourselves. We have to connect to an individual sense of responsibility to bring the values of beloved community into our business dealings. As Dr. King lifted up in a 1966 speech on nonviolence, "Our goal is to create a beloved community and this will require a qualitative change in our souls as well as a quantitative change in our lives."[1] When I think about where we are today and the direction I'm inviting us in, these words from Dr. King feel especially true.

VENTURE's Path to Freedom

When I think about collective action and Black business, I think about VENTURE. VENTURE was an enslaved man living in New England in the late 1700s. He can be thought of as the first Black American founder. Having purchased his own freedom, VENTURE went on to create work for himself and other freedmen in the shipping and transportation business while also working on boat repair and construction. His autobiography, *A Narrative of the Life and Adventures of VENTURE, a Native of Africa: But Resident above Sixty Years in the United States of America*, was published in 1789.[2] In it, he offers his profound firsthand account of life as both a business deal and a business man.

Named Broteer Furro at birth, VENTURE was renamed because his master considered his purchase nothing more than a business venture. VENTURE spelled his name in capital letters in his autobiographical manuscript, and I will do the same.[3] VENTURE was born in 1729 in the region now known as Guinea, a young prince of the Tribe of Dukandarra. He was only six years old when the military occupied his homeland. Thousands of armed men from a foreign White nation supplied neighboring tribes with weapons, equipping and directing them to invade the homelands of others on their behalf. Given that they had been living peacefully for decades, the people of the tribe were not ready for war and were easily defeated.

VENTURE was kidnapped, sold, and enslaved in Rhode Island, where he spent his early years. Sold several times over his lifetime, VENTURE finally lived his later years as a free man in Connecticut. In his autobiography, he writes, "The amount of the money which I had paid my master towards redeeming my time, was seventy-one pounds two shillings. The reason for my master asking such an unreasonable price, was he said, to secure himself in case I should ever come to want. Being thirty-six years old, I left Col. Smith once for all. I had already been sold three different times, made considerable money with seemingly nothing to derive it from, been cheated out of a large sum of money, lost much by misfortunes, and paid an enormous sum for my freedom."[4]

That last sentence breaks my heart wide open. Every word he writes is written so solidly, yet the foundation is shaky; this is a man they tried to break. His words are evidence of the consistent pursuit of profit. This sentence highlights how much everyone benefited financially from VENTURE. It also shows that what is really being sold is access to freedom, and how much it costs to get just one moment of peace.

It took several years for VENTURE to earn the money for his freedom. He worked an additional four years to buy the freedom of his sons, Cuff and Solomon, and then another four years to buy the freedom of his wife, Meg, who was pregnant at the time. In the last pages of his memoir, he looks back on his life, concluding, "I have many consolations; Meg, the wife of my youth, whom I married for love, and bought with my money, is still alive. My freedom is a privilege which nothing else can equal."[58] This is the part of VENTURE's story that is most memorable to me: his purpose in business was never to spend lavishly, but rather to purchase the freedom of his wife and children—to secure his family's ability to be together, to belong to one another. VENTURE's story is the root system of Believe-in-You Money. In his old age, VENTURE owned over 100 acres of land in East Haddam and three houses, a space for each of his children.

Black Founders' Collective Action

It doesn't matter where I am or who I'm asking, Black founders most often explain that freedom is the reason they start their companies. They want the freedom to move how they want to move, to manage schedules how they want to manage them, and to show up for the life they want, not some version of life imagined by a society that excludes and negates their contributions and even their humanity.

I am reminded of how different the experiences and motivations of Black business owners are from those of White business owners. Black business owners are motivated to start their companies because they need income not just for themselves but for the people around them. Black founders are driven by a desire and sense of responsibility to create financial stability that can lead to generational opportunities for their communities and families. This is why I think so many Black founders struggle with the pathway of venture capital. The notion of selling a company for public trade takes them further from the true purpose of their businesses: to provide immediate and sustainable resources for the people around them instead of for some far-off master called the shareholder.

In stark contrast to the venture capital approach, collective action has been foundational for the success of Black people and Black-owned businesses. The history of business using collective action in order to bring more equity and justice is well documented. Jessica Gordon Nembhard's *Collective Courage: A History of African American Cooperative Economic Thought and Practice* is a comprehensive study of the intersections of Black business and collective action.[5] In her work, Nembhard notes how cooperatives have always been important for Black people, as they provided a way to build in spite of the exclusion from mainstream finance and employment. Cooperatives are companies owned by the people that use their services.[6] Cooperative organizations can be federations of workers, farmers, and landowners; mutual insurance companies; or banks and credit unions. As with Believe-in-You Money, the core idea of these entities centers on the intentional pooling of resources and collective action toward more equity.

Since their arrival in America, Black people have always pooled their resources. Sharing resources allows them to grow healthier food, to purchase land, and sometimes to buy tractors and equipment for farming.

"For two centuries they did not earn a regular wage or even own their own bodies, but they often saved what money they could and pooled their savings to help buy their own and one another's freedom,"[7] writes Nembhard. Their efforts also created mutual-aid, burial, and beneficial societies and insurance companies, as well as buying clubs, which were often led by women and connected to religious institutions.[8]

W. E. B. Du Bois referred to the collective work of Black people through the avenue of cooperative business.[9] He described cooperative business as the variety of ways in which Black people shared the costs, risks, and benefits of economic activity. The goal of collective business was to help Black families and communities. And cooperative business, as Du Bois documented, was key in ensuring economic success for Black folks inside of a racist world.

For Black business owners, collective action has always meant that if they wanted safe and fair schools, hospitals, parks, and employment for their own communities, they would not only have to dream it but also pay for it themselves. This meant that after they paid taxes for all the amenities that White people were allowed to enjoy, Black business owners would have to essentially tax themselves again in order to cover the needs in their own communities.

This second tax is sometimes referred to as the Black tax. The Black tax describes the financial support that a professional or entrepreneur of color is obliged to provide to their family and community, outside of their own living expenses, as well as the cost that conscious and unconscious anti-Black discrimination creates. In both instances, the impact of this tax creates a significant financial burden for Black founders and dramatically reduces their ability to build a substantial legacy for future generations.[10] Yet the Black tax has been necessary to sustain Black life in America. Used to build many of the institutions in Black communities across the country, Black collective action and cooperation have been the driving force behind the building of our churches, Boy Scout troops, alumni associations, and even textbooks, school supplies, and teacher salaries.

In 1955, just after the announcement of the Montgomery bus boycott, business leaders met at Dexter Avenue Baptist Church to plan for
an alternate transportation strategy for workers who would be displaced
by the boycott. This was an integral moment for Black business leaders
to join in the collective action of the moment. The city had a large network of Black-owned taxi companies, which provided the first solution
for moving people back and forth around town. But when city officials
learned that this network of Black-owned businesses was providing critical organizational support to the protest, the police began to crack down
on the taxi drivers. That's when Black pharmacist Richard Harris stepped
up and suggested that they initiate a car-pool shuttle service using people's
personal cars, even offering to house the transportation hub at his drug-
store.[11] Without the support of small business, which was the source of
the idea and provided the capacity to create the car-pool strategy, the
boycott would not have succeeded.

With collective action, the issues of injustice and discrimination can
be more effectively addressed in community. Black-owned businesses rely
on the community for their help and protection in the context of unfair
practices and policies. Though the roots of this history are deep, the
promises and challenges of Black collective action continue to this day.
For example, in February 2023, two Black women wanted to open a
nightclub in a commercial space in downtown Mobile, Alabama. After
signing the lease, the women faced six months of delays in getting into
the space because their license to operate was facing significant opposition from the residents who lived near the club. Although the nightclub
was located in the entertainment zone, an area designated for such businesses, and the space had previously housed a club, residents protested
that this club would be too noisy—at least that's what they said in public. During the city council meeting to discuss the license, racist com-
plaints and discriminatory restrictions were levied at the owners. "Is there
an entertainment district on MLK Drive?" read one of the comments

from a neighborhood resident; another comment asked if the business owners were "crackheads" and wanted the owners to take drug tests before they could open.[12] Both comments are dripping with racist assumptions that suggest an intolerance for more than loud noises.

Having a location in the highly sought-after downtown area was a dream for the women, but the delays in opening led to thousands of dollars in accumulated back rent. With no revenue coming in, no clear opening date, and an ongoing battle between the two business owners and local residents, the landlords locked the women out and changed the locks. Nearly ready to give up, the founders reached out to the community in a last-ditch attempt to make something work. Within 30 days they raised $50,000, sourced straight from the community, and enough to keep their business afloat.

If the club owners had followed the old entrepreneur playbook, which says we should go it alone, the business would have remained closed. Instead, they took a different path and experienced the power of Believe-in-You Money in the process, receiving enough financial capital and community support to eventually win the license. The lifeline that community brings can be a breath of fresh air for a business that's being stifled and suffocated by systemic discrimination. When a deep community of customers, friends, and fans are willing to work together for collective change, a company can achieve success against the odds.

Believe-in-You Money and Collective Action

Collective action can happen through formal or informal partnerships; it can create impact inside of cooperative businesses, strategic collaborations, joint venture partnerships, and many other organizational structures. Collective action is a compelling strategy for Black founders because it challenges the go-it-alone culture of the business start-up world, which places unreasonable and unrealistic pressure on a founder to know and do everything themselves. Having to rely on their personal talents, personalities, qualifications, and competencies alone, many founders find that the go-it-alone strategy leads to more stress and burnout.

By engaging in collective action, founders can garner support and momentum from a larger group of people. People rallying together is effective not only in pushing a brand forward but more strategically in bringing important connections to a company when it needs leverage in order to defend itself. Collective action distributes responsibility more broadly across the engaged members of the group, all of whom are now responsible for business outcomes, rather than just the founder. This means that when difficulties arise, there are more people to share in the problem solving and decision making and bring support in overcoming the challenge at hand. And when victories roll in, there are more people to celebrate.

From a Believe-in-You Money perspective, collective action is about how an investment supports economic growth by

- pooling resources,
- defending against discrimination and racial bias, and
- ending burnout and stress.

Think about the term "rugged individualism," which was coined by President Herbert Hoover during the onset of the Great Depression and promotes the idea of embarking on a new frontier with only self-reliance and no government support or aid. The term is a pillar of the narrative of the American dream. This idea, though, is untrue. The reality is that nobody builds a successful company alone.

Collective action matters particularly for Black founders because of their motivations for starting companies. Yes, Black founders start companies because they are incredibly talented creators and innovators and have unique and divinely inspired visions. But sometimes they find themselves in business—and sometimes they've had to hone their creativity and innovation—because they've been marginalized inside and outside of the workforce, shut down, and shut out of opportunities for advancement. Sometimes, they start companies because they see the deterioration of industries around them and the impact that the reduction of opportunities has on their own communities. They may decide that creating a company is a way to address the divestment by bringing needed jobs, skills, and services back to the community. Other times, start-ups are the only option for Black business owners to make a living and support themselves and their families after being targeted and criminalized in the criminal justice system.

There is so much value to be had for Black founders who decide to use collective action versus going it alone. For one thing, working together unlocks more creativity and collaboration. I've witnessed it so many times, including when two of RUNWAY's portfolio companies decided to partner in the midst of the deep heartbreak at the theft of Black lives during the summer of 2020. Essence of Flowers, an Oakland florist shop that is a part of the RUNWAY community, had a beautiful idea to deliver flowers to Black men after the murders of George Floyd and Ahmaud Arbery, as a reminder that they are loved. The volume of response was wonderful and also overwhelming. With so many deliveries to make, Essence of Flowers decided to collaborate with Piikup, a delivery company also in the RUNWAY family. They have since continued working together because it is not only smart for business but also an opportunity to deepen their business relationships and belief in cooperation.

While dominant business culture reinforces the idea that doing "good business" means keeping things close to the chest, we continue to see powerful examples of good, successful, sustainable business as a result of transparency, trust, and cooperation. When we work collectively, network access, reach, and ability to scale all multiply.

Another founder we work with loved her coaching business but hated the day-to-day operational management of the company. During one of our conversations, as she expressed her frustrations, I asked if she was open to collaboration, suggesting that she organize a collective of coaching friends who could all pitch in to get an office manager and social media team member. The idea was successful. Each friend in the collective was able to have their needs met while also saving money as a result of pitching in with a group. Our businesses can grow when we let go of the belief that we have to go it alone.

Believe-in-You Money sees the ways collective responsibility and collective action are inextricably linked to the Black business experience, and it encourages collective work as a way to lessen the load of a founder while also protecting a business from the high risk of encountering racial injustice when interfacing with mainstream institutions. Believe-in-You Money understands that working together in right relationship is not a sign of failure or weakness, but instead an Afro-Indigenous cultural way of ensuring economic sustainability through leveraging the power of the collective.

Why do we need collective action inside of Black business investing? Pastor Andrew said it best: collective action creates "a more democratic—lowercase d—and more creative and collaboration-inducing economy than the one that we all know."

CHAPTER 9

Regenerative versus Exploitative Systems

The first loan I ever attempted to make was to a group of Black farmers in Alabama. Tuskegee University was providing administrative and technical support for the farmers' cooperative, and I was working to provide the debt capital. Even though I spent months doing interviews and codesigning the terms of the loan fund, the farmers were not using the loan product. At the time, I was mystified. I later learned that their reasons for not borrowing money from me were more complex than I could understand.

Mr. Roberts helped to bring me along. Having grown up sharecropping in Sumter County, Alabama, Mr. Roberts was 88 years old when I met him. He worked the land and didn't talk much. But I'm grateful that he supported my growth and learning by telling me about the first and only time he had taken a loan.

When Mr. Roberts was a younger man, the owner of the land where he worked passed away. Mr. Roberts went to talk with the owner's children, who had since moved from the area and gone to the big cities of Atlanta and Birmingham, about the idea of him purchasing some land; he imagined that he could work a small plot and make payments on the land from the produce he sold and from his work as a handyman. The children agreed and told Mr. Roberts to talk with the family banker in neighboring Wilcox County.

So Mr. Roberts did just that. For about 15 years, Mr. Roberts met with the banker, an older White man who was established in the community and thus held a substantial degree of power. Mr. Roberts never missed a payment. He kept a handwritten ledger and knew when his payments would be finished. When that day came, Mr. Roberts met with the banker and asked for his ownership papers. For him, this was about experiencing the sovereignty and agency of a free man. The banker told him to come back another day and he would have them. Mr. Roberts came back a second time and was told the same thing. By the third time, the banker had changed his tune, telling Mr. Roberts, "If you don't get out of here . . ."

The money was gone. There were no papers. He would never be able to confront this man. There would never be a lawsuit. No more words would be spoken on the matter.

I remember thinking that I had done everything right in my approach to loan making in support of the farmers' co-op, including seeking advice and best practices from the most progressive lenders in the country. Yet in the absence of local historical context, I was unconsciously remixing old practices steeped in racism. Further, the act of loan making alone positioned me as a proxy of the not-to-be-trusted banking system, which made community members hesitant to work with me.

I made it my mission to unlearn the lending practices that I thought were right and redirect my focus to structural change. I learned that, in order to be successful, I would have to fully acknowledge Black Americans' historical experiences with both institutional and individual racism within banking and finance. I would have to listen and understand the depth of the terror that has led Black people to be one of the least trusting groups in America when it comes to financial institutions. If I wanted to bring more capital to Black companies, I would have to fundamentally change how I understood investments, which meant I would also have to intentionally dismantle the racist ideas I inherited simply by living in a racist system—even as a Black person with my own experiences of racism. Only after dismantling these ideas could I develop and engage in alternative systems and practices that embody the acknowledgment of our history and the context in which our economy exists. From there, we can make way for a new paradigm.

I learned all of this from Mr. Roberts.

If you are Black and at any point have tried to farm in the South, you've been discriminated against. Through discriminatory lending practices and deliberate delays in financial support, the USDA (United States Department of Agriculture) routinely blocked critical federal funds from generations of Black farmers. As Black farmers' debts began to mount, millions of acres were put at risk, and White buyers swooped in and snapped them up. In 1920, the number of Black Americans engaged in farming peaked at nearly one million, constituting 14 percent of all farmers at the time. But by 1997, they had lost 90 percent of their property. By contrast, White farmers had lost only 2 percent of their property in the same period. As of 2017, there were just 35,470 Black-owned farms, representing only 1.7 percent of all farms in the United States.[1]

The National Black Farmers Association, which represents Black agriculture businesses, has filed lawsuits against the federal government for the estimated loss of $326 billion of land in America owing to discrimination during the twentieth century.[2] The most notable of these lawsuits were the Pigford cases against the USDA in 1999. These cases acknowledged the government's history of discrimination in two lawsuits settled in 1999 and 2010, which together made thousands of Black farmers eligible for over $2 billion collectively.[3] The cases went on for so long that many of the original claimants died before the claims were honored.

The legacy of racism embedded in the Pigford cases continues to drive legal proceedings in the present. As recently as 2022, Black farmers filed suit against the government for failure to deliver on promised capital. During the COVID-19 pandemic, the government promised $4 billion in debt relief in exchange for their continued production and distribution of food throughout the global crisis. But again, the debt relief was repealed, leaving Black farmers facing the familiar threat of widespread foreclosure, even after helping the nation endure one of the most challenging and life-threatening periods of American history.

Black farmers are the canary in the coal mine; they've experienced the true personal and economic impacts of racial discrimination in America, and they have stories to share. I'm grateful for the wisdom Black farmers bring to our thinking about the Black-owned business experience. I have always found these business owners to be thoughtful and careful with the gifts of the resources around them. Black farmers possess a wisdom that reminds them—and inspires me—to never take more than they can manage or make use of, and to always plan for the future. By observing Black farmers, I've learned about interdependence and regenerative practices that center whole-systems thinking and teach us that everything in the universe is organized into systems whose interlinked parts work together as a whole. These ideas are not new; they are Afro-Indigenous ways of seeing systems. By reengaging with this ancestral, time-tested thinking in the finance space, we can evolve our economic system into one that is more capable of taking care of the many rather than working for the benefit of the few.

Nature-Informed Systems

Regeneration means putting life back into the system rather than simply extracting what serves us without attending to the maintenance of balance. Regenerative systems create value for everyone in the ecosystem, which helps the overall system operate more holistically and for the long term. Such systems honor that the world is built around reciprocal and coevolutionary relationships, where humans, other living beings, and all elements of an ecosystem rely on and connect to one another for well-being. They recognize that addressing the interconnected social and environmental challenges we face relies on rebalancing and restoring the interconnectedness of our relationships. When applied to our economy, regenerative thinking can be a source of growth, creativity, and innovation, unlocking the potential for greater community wealth and more widespread democratic participation.

In the context of Believe-in-You Money, regeneration means applying a life-giving strategy to the way we finance Black founders. We need an approach that values the dignity of work and the full humanity of workers and prioritizes shared governance and ownership of work and resources. We need to dismantle the existing oppressive systems that devalue people and their labor and inspire violence and wealth-hoarding by a few through extraction and exploitation of the many. We need investments in Black companies that look to create local production and manufacturing and that create pathways for workers to earn the wages and equity that they need to build generational wealth. Regenerative practices help us think about the types of investments we need to make if we want to shift the wealth outcomes of Black people, as part of shifting the overall ecosystem.

Konda Mason helps me better understand regeneration as applied to business. I am lucky to have Konda in my life. She is the founder of Jubilee Justice, a social enterprise that leverages reparative genealogy and regenerative agriculture to heal and transform the wounds suffered by the people and the land. Jubilee Justice uses learning journeys, which bring together diverse groups of change makers to invest in Black farmers' ability to build sustainable, regenerative practices; cooperative ownership; and financial security. And I couldn't think of a better person than Konda to consult for my chapter on moving toward regenerative financial systems and away from exploitative, extractive ones.

Konda reminds us that regenerative agriculture—much like Believe-in-You Money—is another opportunity to return to Afro-Indigenous practices that were more widespread before industrialization. "If you look at Afro-Indigenous farming practices," Konda says, "it is what people are calling regenerative agriculture. It's our heritage—the Indigenous folks, Black folks—this is how we've been farming from the beginning. And it's come around full circle."

Konda also serves as strategic adviser for my company, RUNWAY, and has helped us integrate a regenerative systemic approach for investing in Black companies. "Asking a systemic question," she says, "is the only way to find the acupuncture point—something that can make it shift." When we first met, Konda was the director of Impact Hub Oakland, a gathering place for social entrepreneurs and economic innovators looking to make the world more sustainable and just. In this space, surrounded by a trove of business owners, Konda conducted an anecdotal research project to learn more about start-up funding—who was getting it and how much it was costing. The unsurprising pattern of Black founders having to pay more severe penalties on their debt capital informed our approach with RUNWAY lending.

While the average market rate cost for the types of loans RUNWAY makes is usually somewhere between 7 and 10 percent, we're consistently lending between 0 and 3 percent. We understand that if we want to restore what was strategically denied to and stripped from Black people, we can't continue to extract from those same people at the same rates. If we want to support the closure of the racial wealth gap, something's got to give. Regenerative capital takes all this into consideration. Guided by Konda's expertise in this area, RUNWAY embedded a reparative approach into the design of our loan making, the ways our company operated, and even how our funds were underwritten—by community, in a way that allowed us to become the friends-and-family round of capital that Black companies so needed and deserved.

Regenerative Finance

Slow Money, a membership network that pools members' money to make 0-percent loans to organic farms and small food enterprises, introduced me to regenerative finance.[4] Members focus their investments in agriculture, food, and soil projects all over the United States and in a few international locations. As the name suggests, Slow Money's aim is to slow down the pace of money and focus it on things that matter—like our food systems. This network understands that money can move too fast, companies can be too big, and finance can be too complex and that a simpler, holistic strategy for growth and investing can be found by studying nature.[5]

The concept of regenerative economics was made popular in the paper *Regenerative Capitalism: How Universal Principles and Patterns Will Shape Our New Economy* by John Fullerton.[6] When he wrote the paper, Fullerton was leaving a successful Wall Street career with JPMorgan Chase and wanted to see whether a holistic economic strategy could be drawn from what we know about science, living systems, and ecological traditions. Since then, regenerative economics, which brings nature's laws and patterns of systemic health, self-organization, self-renewal, and regenerative vitality into socioeconomic systems, has brought together a rich and diverse field of investors. Across a broad range of access points and industries, regenerative finance has found a home in the hearts of people who want to repair the extractive economy. What connects these very different communities, all committed to regenerative finance, is a belief in its promising ability to nurture stable, healthy, and sustainable systems.

In an interview in *Forbes* magazine, Jasper van Brakle, president of RSF Social Finance (which is a financial partner to RUNWAY), discusses RSF's movement toward regenerative finance. "The time for regenerative finance is now," he said. "We can no longer hide from systemic racism, growing inequality or the climate emergency that impacts everyone—

although not everyone equally."[7] RSF believes capital markets can play a critical role in making restoration, regeneration, and healing possible at scale. RSF's goal is to take the emphasis off of accumulation of money as the desired outcome of an investment and instead move money as a tool that facilitates circulation, rather than simply and irresponsibly extracting maximum financial profit.

In the Web3-decentralized-autonomous-organization-blockchain world, regenerative finance (or ReFi as it's often called in these spaces) promises to take decentralized technology systems and give them purpose and meaning. ReFi wants to use money as a tool to solve systemic problems by changing the underlying circumstances that drive our current economic model. By building on smart contracts and blockchain technology, the need for financial intermediaries to ensure fairness and trust is gone. The hope is that, with a different and more intentional set of foundational rules, the system can transform into something different and more intentional. Instead of a system that values the accumulation of money at the expense of people and the planet, ReFi uses capital to create healthy and equitable social and environmental systems.

Like Believe-in-You Money, ReFi can focus on investment approaches as intentional strategies for achieving change. This promising strategy is finding an audience all over the globe because it is going beyond environmental, social, and governance measurements (which tend to focus more on reducing negative impacts than on creating positive ones) and pushing beyond impact investing (which tends to have very narrow targets). Even with its expansive vision, ReFi can only achieve its goals most powerfully if applied through a directly antiracist and power-building framework. Such a framework can ground the movement in an awareness of how outcomes are created and who is benefiting; and without it, ReFi runs the risk of continuing to leave vulnerable communities behind. Pairing ReFi with a Believe-in-You-Money approach can honor the intersectionality of environmental degradation and racism as connected ideas that must be addressed together.

Reconnecting with the Land

Konda speaks to the disconnect that our current state of industrialization creates. "The way people are farming these days," she shares, "they are on big tractors and they never even touch the earth." She explains that getting closer to the land, closer to its magic and power, supports the healing of this disconnect. "If you want to get involved in these ways of dealing with the land and with farming, you have to get more intimate, you have to get more proximate, you have to touch the earth, you have to have a relationship." And the same applies, she says, if we want to heal the disconnect among people. "Regeneration asks us to get into a place of depth and intimacy when working with Black founders."

Believe-in-You Money and regeneration have in common the invitation to come back into right relationship. Right relationship looks for opportunities for cooperation and holistic interactions, and values humanity as an integral part of life, acknowledging that there is no real separation between "us" and "it." It is also about remembering what is sacred—a parallel to my conversation with Brendan Martin about identifying what's sacred in our understanding and definition of risk. Konda reflects, "If we look at the rivers and the oceans and the eagles and even the so-called weeds, we see that it is all about understanding what is sacred. The earth and its inhabitants and what grows here is all sacred. And so it requires us to become more intimate and more proximate to the people and planet's needs. By taking a regenerative approach, we are setting out to practice and strategize around protecting what is sacred." We are all connected to one another, and, as a result, damage to any part of the system will ripple back to harm every other part as well. And healing any part of the system will similarly work to benefit the whole.

Konda talks about the sacred as "believing in the things that you cannot see." She teases this out for us, saying, "Look at the soil. What we see is a tree. We see a bush. We see a plant. We see a flower. But underneath the soil, there's a whole world going on underneath there." And while dominant contemporary ways of thinking emphasize the value of that which we can prove with data, facts, and rational information, regeneration requires something different. Believe-in-You Money requires something different. As Konda says about regenerative agriculture or Afro-Indigenous farming, "Not only do you have to begin to understand and believe that which you cannot see with the naked eye; you have to also start to love it. Because this is how life happens."

Our current financial system encourages, rewards, and increases inequality, exploitation, and violence against marginalized people and the land. If we want to shift our path and our reality, we need to trust that another way is truly possible, even though we can't see the tangible evidence before us just yet. We need to advance regenerative investments that embody a love of Black people. I often hear people say that systems change is too hard, but if we remember that we are the system, and the system is us, we better understand that it can, in fact, be changed. As Anu Gupta elevated in my conversation with him, "The system isn't some amorphous blob outside in the world. It is a structure of ideas, beliefs, actions, ways of being that are upheld by our individual choice to uphold them." This means that the change we seek can also start at the individual level.

But we must move from a place of love. As my conversation with Konda was closing, she emphasized love as the core of this work. "Love is the glue that brings it all together," she said, "because it is a system. We compartmentalize it as if it's separate and it's not. It is all one big, beautiful system."

CHAPTER 10

Are You Believing Yet?

believe
bĭ-lēv´
intransitive verb
To accept as true or real.
To credit with veracity.
To expect or suppose; think.

Believe in . . . Possibility

I'm asking folks to believe. To believe that there is a way through the history of this country. To believe that there is something better for us collectively. To believe that healing is available to us, and to invest our resources, our hearts, our whole bodies and selves into that belief. I'm asking us—even in the absence of full, tangible proof that everything could change—to believe that something more beautiful is possible.

I believe that together we can move away from extractive capital practices and toward alternatives that honor Black business owners' time, talents, labor, art, and rituals. I believe that every system that was created can be changed. And I believe not only that change is possible but that *we are the people to do it*. We must acknowledge that, within existing systems and institutions, there are individual people who care—people like you and me who want to repair the impacts of racial bias and end the racial wealth gap for good, and who understand that changing the way we approach investing in Black companies is necessary in order to do so.

When I tell the story of Black business ownership in America, I feel like I'm telling my own story. Early on in my journey, I was a burned-out entrepreneur and simultaneously a relentless investor who saw a huge gap in capital offerings and lack of support for the incredible talent around me. I wish someone would have told me back then that not getting capital was not about me or my ability but about the systemic racism that was still at work. Perhaps with that understanding, I would have had more compassion for myself when I heard the chorus of early "nos." I hope this book constantly reminds Black founders, innovators, and creators like me that we are not the cause of the patterned denial of financial support we experience; we are deserving, and we are a part of the solution. We *all* are.

Because there has not been a moment in Black American history absent of intentional financial sabotage, we have to admit that—if we claim to be committed to racial justice and ending systemic anti-Blackness—changing course is the best thing we can do. During my conversation with Konda Mason, much of which appeared in the previous chapter, she said, "If you think about it, the financial system is at the core of all the other systems: the education system, the medical system, the incarceration system—the financial system is underneath all of that." She went on to talk about the impact of this reality, saying, "To starve Black people of funding is a way of moving them through all the other systems. It shapes who's going to end up in jail, who's going to end up incarcerated, who's going to end up with medical diseases at an extraordinary rate. When you starve people from resources, it has all these other impacts and results."

The impact of racism on economics is staggering and widely affects every part of the Black business experience. Take the water crisis in Jackson, Mississippi, for instance. After heavy rainfall in August 2022, the infrastructure failed, exacerbating a preexisting water crisis, which in turn shuttered businesses and crippled the city's economy. This wasn't the first time that the water system failed, but the city had never experienced a disaster like this, which went on for months. Jackson is 80 percent Black. This crisis was not a sudden coincidence but rather the result of historical and systemic racial disinvestment and disadvantaging. The environmental racism that Jackson residents and business owners experienced was about which communities get financial resources and which ones get left behind. Withholding financial resources from Black communities is about wielding power in the interest of inequity, and its detrimental impacts reach far beyond the intended community. In fact, discriminatory financing compromises our interconnectedness as well as the integrity of our supposed democracy.

The six grounding ideas of *Believe-in-You Money* are what we need to balance power and lovingly invest in Black-owned businesses. By adopting goals around transformation, shared and equitable risk, restorative and mutual benefit, transparency, interdependence, and regeneration, we can create experiences that unlock spaciousness and a sense of belonging for Black founders. When we do this, we set ourselves up to move in right relationship with one another. As Sonya Renee Taylor reminds us, being in right relationship returns us to a place of radical self-love, where we understand the inherent value, dignity, and worth of all people, starting with ourselves. When we move from this place, we naturally establish nonextractive relationships because we do not need others to be at a deficit in order for us to feel whole. The ideas in *Believe-in-You Money* are powerful not only for supporting Black-owned businesses but for everyone who wants a more restorative economy.

Believe in . . . Healing

During my time at RUNWAY, I've learned that in order to be successful in financing Black companies, one has to fully acknowledge Black

Americans' historical experiences with both institutional and individual racism. Trying to move as if this history is not a factor is regressive and deeply harmful. The good news is that things are changing for Black founders. I'm seeing foundation leaders, bank CEOs, and wealth holders listening and stepping up to challenge the status quo, pushing for the redistribution of wealth and restoration of land back to Black and Indigenous communities.

Konda and I have the opportunity to work with wealth holders who are clear that they have to re-Indigenize their money practices, stripping away all remnants of colonialism from the way they do business, if they hope to achieve systemic change. "To be here now, and to have this legacy of survival and thriving," Konda reflects, "to have this onslaught of resources that are turning towards Black folks—I'm seeing it. I'm a living example of it. It's just a wonderful thing to see—to be able to partner but not be exploitative, to have real relationships. That's what it takes. It takes creating relationships and not transactions. This world is so transactional, and that's not how we roll. When you come in with right relationship, there are resources, and we can partner, then we can get something done." We need more wealthy investors who operate with the foundational understanding that their high net worth isn't a reflection of their more deserving or harder-working nature; rather, it's a result of generational privilege, some of which came as a direct result of extracting capital from Black people, Black bodies, and Black brilliance.

Believe-in-You Money has helped me listen to Black founders, and when I do, I hear their inspirational successes alongside the challenges they face while navigating the financial system. Listening is at the heart of getting into right relationship. Building intentional right relationships with people can reshape the power dynamics and heal wounded relationships with money resources too. As I listen, I hear how much healing matters to Black founders. The pain of the past—and present—echoes through their reflections, underscoring the importance of acknowledging, honoring, and remedying the institutional injustices that have terrorized our communities, our families, and our businesses. If we want to repair the impacts of financial exclusion, then we have to center the healing of these wounds in all the relationships, investments, and structures we build.

During my interviews for the book, I asked each person if they have ever personally received Believe-in-You Money. I knew that each of them was involved in moving money, but it's a very different thing to have been on the receiving end of this kind of capital. Each time I prompted someone to think about their Believe-in-You Money story, the energy shifted. I saw eyes light up and reflections of joy and encouragement as they shared the details. Sonya shared, "My life is filled with Believe-in-You Money. I can't even language how blessed I've been. My life is a result of people saying, 'I believe in you, and I'm going to invest in you.'" She went on to offer the specifics of how this support manifested for her. "I started Buy Back Black Debt in 2020 to pay off student loan debt. I had $118,000 worth of student loans. And I had fantasized all kinds of ways that this money was going to disappear. I fantasized that one day I was just gonna become so rich, and I was gonna walk in and write them a check and sign. But we coordinated the Buy Back Black Debt campaign, and over the course of 16 weeks, over 6,000 people donated and cleared $118,000 worth of my student debt." This monumental, no-strings-attached, Believe-in-You investment transformed Sonya's reality. "I ugly cried that day. Something was altered in space-time. From thinking of myself as the broke student with a ton of debt, putting myself through school, navigating a parent with addiction, and all of this trauma—all of a sudden, that thing that I had so convinced myself I had to do alone, it was like 6,000 people came behind me and were like, 'We're going to actually go back and walk with you through this entire experience.'" Sonya's story spoke so clearly to the power of Believe-in-You Money, and she offered a beautiful sentiment as she closed, saying, "Believe-in-You Money has the power to go back and heal the traumas that people thought were never going to be healed."

Sonya's words illuminate the gift of experiencing Believe-in-You Money. And yet, when I think about how wonderful Believe-in-You Money is, and as much as I believe Black founders need it, I know we are still at a place in time where, for many of us, it feels impossible to imagine. I ask the question about what an economy that loves Black people looks like because I know that we can only create something if we can first envision it. When I ask the question, it is unsurprisingly met with long pauses. Could it even happen? Can we quiet the pain of the past enough to imagine beyond it? Konda didn't feel sure of the possibility in the present. "I have to tell you, Jessica, this country? An economy that loves Black people? The seeds aren't there," she offered, staying true to her agricultural grounding. "Capitalism don't love nothing but more of itself. That's what capitalism loves: more capitalism. Maybe once we compost a whole lot of people, you know, and grow a whole new crop, then maybe we can create an economy that loves Black people. We can certainly move in that direction now, but we have to heal backwards in order to heal forwards. We can't pretend that this didn't happen, that this history is not here."

Believe in . . . Black Joy

I feel what Konda is saying. There can be no future economy that loves Black people if we are not willing to be honest about the history of the enslavement and genocide of African and Indigenous people, and then allow that honesty to guide the transformation of our systems. And while it is, of course, crucial to interrogate and remedy the pain, there is something equally transformational and liberating to be found inside of Black joy.

Black joy is a healing balm. It has the power to break down and break through the cruelty produced from our economic realities. Black joy reminds us that we have agency to infuse love into our circumstances, our experiences, and even our systems. So while we *do* need the world to get behind our joy and invest in ways that support it, we do *not* have to wait for them to notice us or give us permission to shine. Sonya elevated this idea, saying, "Black joy is so indifferent to whatever the extenuating circumstances of the world are. Black joy just is. I describe it like the sun." She continued, "Everybody could be tripping, and if the sun is gonna shine, it's gonna shine, period. Clouds rolling, they might try to obscure it; rain might come, storms, but that hasn't stopped the sun from shining." Konda gets this, too. She understands the relationship between the glory and resilience of Black people and the oppressions we've experienced, and she provokes us to reflect on how much we've been able to accomplish—to keep our own sun shining—in light of countless seemingly insurmountable barriers and attacks. "Who would we be? What would be our situation, really," she asked, "if we did not live with racially based obstacles? I wonder where White folks would be if we didn't have racially based obstacles, too. It would be another world."

If we truly want this other world to be possible—if we want Black business owners to have a radically different experience than what they have now—we will need to access Black joy to get there. What I love about Black joy is that it's our own lane from which to draw resources, make plans, and change the game. Through the lens of Black joy I am free to imagine a world of beautiful possibilities that suddenly make real the joy that Sonya talks about. What comes to pass when we transform the economy into one that loves Black people is an exciting invitation to imagine, actively practice, and work toward a world of healed people and places.

In Anu Gupta's vision of an economy that loves Black people, "every single school in this country would be well resourced with technology, with education, with books and resources, meals that are healthy and nourishing." He added, "We wouldn't have a system of criminal punishment. Rather, we would have a system of restoration and healing." When we believe that we can move away from an extractive economic system, we are in turn believing that a beautiful future of healing and restoration is available. A future that, instead of providing some children with a wealth of opportunities while denying others of essential resources, offers equitable conditions and access for all children, as well as a high quality of life that is evenly distributed across diverse demographics.

Nwamaka Agbo asked a poignant and pointed question: "If we do believe in interdependence, if we do believe in our collective liberation, then what are we doing?" She continued, "The work that Nikole Hannah-Jones has done shows us that the ways that we think about the economy are just equations made up by people—and particularly made up by White men—to reflect their needs and interests."[1] Nwamaka's work with the Restorative Economies Fund took a different path. "We took a chance," she said, "to see if we could actually take the restorative economics framework and use it for a due diligence tool or a term sheet that reflected these ideas of Black joy, that reflected what it looks like to ensure that communities are able to live and thrive with dignity." And they succeeded, making it clear to Nwamaka that "the question is not, 'Is it possible?' It's, 'Do we actually have the political will? Are people committed to doing the hard and necessary work to figure out how we move money differently, so that we are all able to live with dignity and so that we can thrive?'"

When I think of all that is possible when we believe that we can—all that our collective dignity and shared ability to thrive entails—I am emboldened by the power that's waiting to be unleashed. Instead of transactional capital and a deeply inequitable society, we can commit to human exchanges that remind us of our interconnectedness and work toward a shared reality that reflects this understanding. Instead of going it alone, we can work together to dismantle racism and build generational wealth, power, and leadership within Black and Brown communities.

Believe-in-You Money offers guidance for a movement of people on this reparative finance journey to fix the wrongs of racism, patriarchy, and capitalism for Black companies and for all of us. A movement that takes a radical approach toward changing the face of who moves money and how it is moved. A movement with its eyes set on the goal of wealth redistribution that creates the conditions for healing and repair to follow. We believe that the capital experience should see the fullness of Black founders, understand their visions, and move in concert with them over the lifetimes of their careers, and that—despite the damaging history we continue to navigate—this different reality is possible.

Believe in . . . Worthiness

> *Economic justice is about the ancestral*
> *legacies of a people.*
> —Elandria Williams

Meeting Elandria Williams was like winning the lottery. I'd found someone who nerded out on the same things that I loved: the South, economic justice, and community building. Elandria (she/they) was a force to be reckoned with; her intellect was unmatched, and she was deeply respected in solidarity economy and workers' rights movements. We met at Highlander Research and Education Center in New Market, Tennessee. Highlander is an idyllic setting made for global change makers. Surrounded by the rolling hills of the Appalachian mountains and flanked by orchard trees, it was our own Hogwarts. The center has been and continues to be the educational home base for revolutionary leaders from all over the world, including Dr. Martin Luther King Jr., Rosa Parks, and present-day movement leaders.

In 2009, I was at Highlander, studying nonviolent organizing with Dr. Bernard Lafayette in my new role as board member, when Elandria walked into the room. She was the education and youth leader at Highlander, and that day she was recruiting people to help her move books from the Septima Clark Library to a new, more secure location. I remember how excited we both were to be holding rare papers of the organizing movement. We definitely did a lot of oohing and aahing that day. This was how our friendship began, rooted in the joy and brilliance of our ancestors' good work.

Elandria was a modern-day abolitionist with an understanding that the throughline fueling slavery, prison, and punishment was an economy that was built on stolen and exploited labor. Elandria committed her time to workers' rights, determined to see the end of the practice of extracting from people and the planet, a value she learned early in church. Growing up in the Tennessee Valley Unitarian Universalist Church in Knoxville, Tennessee, Elandria tapped into a sense of faith that inspired her to work tirelessly toward building an inclusive, antioppressive world where we are all held inside of a circle of love and care.

All that Elandria learned, she shared. I once heard her give a beautiful definition of the word "economy" that sticks with me to this day. She said an economy is simply "how you take care of home." An economy is the ways people spend money and the ways people make money, which together are essentially all the things we do to take care of home. Elandria taught us that an economy can be big or small, local or global, and either extractive or compassionate. During an interview with the Democracy Collaborative, Elandria explained that "local economies by themselves are not progressive. A plantation is a local economy. So the question cannot be avoided of who controls the economy."[2] This part—ownership of the economy and the power to determine how it functions—was something that both Elandria and I understood as foundational to building democracy and why we always linked around my work to support Black-owned businesses.

Elandria would have been the first person I called to interview for this book if she hadn't passed away unexpectedly on September 23, 2020. I relied on E (as many friends called her) to ground me in the work, trusting that she would challenge me to make sure I considered and included everyone in my analysis. Because I could not invite E into a real-time conversation to articulate and elevate—as she so often and so skillfully did—why we need the subject of *Believe-in-You Money*, I wanted to include her voice in this book in a different way. In honor of my friend and now ancestor, I share below a poem about worthiness that E posted on her Facebook page just weeks before she transitioned.

Worthiness is at the heart of Believe-in-You Money. It is through radical love for ourselves, as Sonya talks about earlier in the book, that we come to understand and believe that we are worthy, right now, to receive love. There is nothing we have to do to be "deserving," and there is nothing that we must do to fit in. We are *all* worthy of an economy that loves Black people. To access any improved reality, beyond the history and the impact of the present context, we must decide that we are worthy of a repaired economy; Believe-in-You Money is one way we can get there.

I'm sharing Elandria's full poem here, with all her power and purpose, with the hopes that you feel inspired to join this revolution for change.

"We Are Worthy"

We are worthy
Not because of what we produce
But because of who we are
We are divine bodies of light and darkness
You are not worthy because of what you offer, not because of
*   what is in your mind, not for the support you give others,*
*   not for what you give at all*
We are worthy and are whole just because
In this great turning, in this great pandemic, in this radical
*   readjustment and alignment*
We are not disposable, we are needed, we are the very people
*   that have withstood everything that has been thrown at*
*   us as a people and as Maya Angelou would say*
Still I Rise
We arise from the pain

We rise from the grief

We arise from the limits people place on us and the limits we place on ourselves

We rise to be the children and the ancestors

We rise to be our true selves

Our true selves in relationship to our families and communities

Recognizing our liberating and whole selves

Honoring them and others as we strive for abundant communities, abundant lives, abundant relationships, and abundant values and cultural manifestations

We are worthiness personified

I, you, and we are worthy and deserve a life where we are not always fighting for our existence

Imagine what we could create if we were not always in the struggle

Imagine what we could envision if we could just be let to just go there

So tired of always having to resist, to fight, demanding, pushing

To everyone that has the courage, the power, the ability to co-create what we want and need while rooting in what we can't lose and who we are

You are the visionary

You are the hope

You are our ancestors' dreams

No you might not ever end up on some list somewhere

But you are on a list in someone's heart and mind

And if it's in how you move in the world so people can see by example

You are the embodiment of what we need

Thanks to all that are the embodiment

The embodiment not of productivity but the embodiment of
   radical love, care, and sanctuary
It's time
Embodiment time
Embodiment
Living one's values out loud
Let me everyday live my values out loud
Let us everyday live our values out loud
Embodying our values
Not the productivity quotient
Beyond productivity
Past productivity
True embodiment
Life³

—by Elandria Williams

Elandria's potent words remind me that everything we need is in our bones. The power to change the world is inside of us. Inside of me. Inside of you. We have to believe it's possible, and we have to have the courage to act. I give thanks to E's parents, Erven and Elnora Williams, for pouring into me and our whole community the same tenacity and pursuit for justice that they poured into Elandria; we are forever changed in the best ways.

Ending extractive capital lending to Black companies is the right thing to do. Black founders should not have to continue to endure the instability and perpetual survival mode that come with the lack of financial security. They need and deserve a break from always having to be resilient in the face of repeated financial trauma; it's time to show some love so that Black founders can experience the rest and assurance they need in order to truly unleash the full impact of Black brilliance in our society. When I think of the opportunity in front of us, to change the system, to change our future, I hear the words of Assata Shakur: "I believe that a lost ship, steered by tired, seasick sailors, can still be guided home to port." As someone who's endured experiences that would render most people entirely hopeless, Assata still believes in the ripe possibility of a brighter future. I believe with her, and I invite you to believe too.

Believe-in-You Money
Discussion Guide

*B*elieve-in-You Money: What Would It Look Like If the Economy Loved
Black People shines a light on the many ways we all invest in and receive Believe-in-You Money. Whether you provide support, financial or
otherwise, to a Black founder with an amazing idea that needs investment
or you prioritize supporting Black-owned brands or organizations in your
daily life, you are an investor in Black imagination and joy, and perhaps
even an antiracist investor.

As you read the book, feel free to explore the chapters that call to
you. The stories shared and leaders highlighted demonstrate what Believe-
in-You Money can do—and is already doing—to accelerate repair, restoration, and a fundamental reimagining of our economy.

Please note that the book and questions are informed by perspectives
and experiences grounded in the Global North. The storytelling pulls
from the author's life in Chicago and Alabama and gleans insights from
efforts across the globe, like the cooperative movement in Europe, worker
ownership and entrepreneurship in South and Central America, and deep
systemic healing and regenerative agriculture across the American South.
Acknowledging the ancestors and wisdom keepers who have informed
and led this work for decades is a consistent thread.

The following questions are meant to deepen your thinking around Believe-in-You Money as you spend time with the book. They are structured at three levels: individual, community, and our shared systems.

Individual

1. Who shaped your relationship to money? How did you learn about the value of money?
2. What is a moment when someone believed in you and invested in you?
3. What is a moment when you believed in someone else and supported them financially?
4. How does it feel to recognize yourself as an investor?
5. How do you think about risk when it comes to money? What do you consider the "thing you cannot lose"? Whose risk do you center? The investor's? The entrepreneur's? The risk to future generations?
6. Have you ever experienced shame or fear around money?
7. What are some of your favorite examples of investing in Black joy?
8. Whom can you talk with as you consider how you might activate more Believe-in-You Money?
9. Can you imagine yourself as an antiracist investor? How do you invest to directly address the racial wealth gap?
10. When you imagine being an antiracist investor, does it help you understand risk in a new way? How?

Community

1. What are some of the qualities you observe in a transformational (not transactional) relationship? How do those relationships feel?
2. What are some examples of the racial wealth gap that you have seen or experienced? How does gender intersect with race and wealth?

3. Have you been part of a group or community that invests Believe-in-You Money? If so, which one?

4. How can we reimagine risk, as we repair our connection to one another and to the planet, while centering Black people?

5. What can companies and organizations do to identify and dismantle violence and oppression in their business practices?

6. When you imagine using capital to repair and restore your community, what comes to mind? Where is Believe-in-You Money most needed?

7. When you think of people who use their money to make positive change, who or what do they prioritize? How do they activate Believe-in-You Money for the greater good?

8. What are some examples of collective giving and action translating to real change in your community?

9. How can we collectively embrace and nurture Black imagination? What are examples of a community investing in Black imagination and creativity?

10. Is there someone in your network who would benefit from Believe-in-You Money right now? What steps could you take to make that happen?

Shared Systems

1. What would it look like if the economy loved Black people? What outcomes could this have?

2. What is an example of when you experienced the financial system as overly complicated or unfair?

3. If everyday people are investors, what does that suggest about our collective power?

4. What if, instead of considering money the most important thing in a financial transaction, we prioritized the creator or founder? How would entrepreneurship look different than it does today?

5. What financial terms would encourage us to consider risk in a more holistic way?

6. How can nonextractive, antiracist financing begin to repair the harm of generations of exploitation? Do you know of any financial institutions that are doing this work?

7. Have you been exposed to distributed ownership models like cooperatives? If so, how have you witnessed their ability to transform not only individual lives but also local and regional economies?

8. What would it look like to have an economy built on antiracist investing?

9. How can business standards evolve to create systems that are more equitable, inclusive, and just? What kinds of norms should businesses adopt?

10. What would an antiracist world look, feel, and sound like?

Notes

Preface

1. Stewart, S., III, Chui, M., Manyika, J., Julien, J. P., Hunt, D. V., Sternfels, B., Woetzel, J., & Zhang, H. (2022, July 14). *The Economic State of Black America: What Is and What Could Be*. McKinsey & Company.
2. *Availability of Credit to Small Businesses—September 2017*. (n.d.). Board of Governors of the Federal Reserve System. Retrieved December 1, 2022, from https://www.federalreserve.gov /publications/2017-september-availability-of-credit-to-small-businesses.htm; Davis, D.-M. (2023, January 6). *Black Founders Still Raised Just 1% of All VC Funds in 2022*. TechCrunch. https://techcrunch.com/2023/01/06/black-founders-still-raised-just-1-of-all-vc-funds-in-2022/

Introduction

1. *Still Building: ProjectDiane 2021 Update*. (n.d.). Digitalundivided. Retrieved January 14, 2023, from https://www.digitalundivided.com/reports/still-building-project-diane-2021-update
2. Parker, K., Horowitz, J., & Mahl, B. (2016). *On Views of Race and Inequality, Blacks and Whites Are Worlds Apart*. Pew Research Center.
3. Lahr, D., Adams, A., Edges, A., & Bletz, J. (2022, August). Where Do We Go from Here? The Survival and Recovery of Black-Owned Businesses Post-COVID-19. *Humanity & Society* 46(3), 460–77. https://doi.org/10.1177/01605976211049243. PMCID: PMC8784976; Fairlie, R. (2020). The Impact of COVID-19 on Small Business Owners: Continued Losses and Partial Rebound in May 2020. Working Paper No. 2020-01, UC Santa Cruz, Institute for Social Transformation. https://transform.ucsc.edu/wp-content /uploads/2020/06/WP2020-01_Fairlie.pdf
4. Perez, F. (2022, April 27). *How Do We Build Black Wealth? Understanding the Limits of Black Capitalism*. Nonprofit Quarterly. https://nonprofitquarterly.org/how-do-we-build -black-wealth-understanding-the-limits-of-black-capitalism/
5. *Building Power*. (n.d.). The Praxis Project. Retrieved December 1, 2022, from https://www .thepraxisproject.org/building-power
6. King, M. L., Jr. (n.d.). Where Do We Go from Here? In *Annual Report*. 11th Convention of the Southern Christian Leadership Conference, Atlanta, Georgia. https://kinginstitute .stanford.edu/where-do-we-go-here

7. Solomon, A., & Rankin, K. (2019). *How We Fight White Supremacy: A Field Guide to Black Resistance* (Illustrated). Bold Type Books, p. 213.

8. Ibid., p. 214.

9. The New School. (2015, October 12). *bell hooks: Moving from Pain to Power I The New School* [Video]. YouTube. https://www.youtube.com/watch?v=cpKuLl-GC0M

Chapter 1

1. *Henry Boyd's Manufacturing Company.* (n.d.). National Museum of African American History & Culture. Retrieved January 4, 2023, from https://www.searchablemuseum.com/henry-boyds-manufacturing-company/

2. Woodson, C. G. (1916). The Negroes of Cincinnati Prior to the Civil War. *The Journal of Negro History, 1*(1), 1–22. https://doi.org/10.2307/2713512

3. Collins, K. (2014). *The Nature of Investing: Resilient Investment Strategies through Biomimicry* (1st ed.). Routledge.

4. RSF Social Finance. Racial Justice Collaborative. Retrieved January 11, 2023, from https://rsfsocialfinance.org/give/give-to-rsf/racial-justice-collaborative/; Acumen. Retrieved January 4, 2023, from https://acumen.org/about/

Chapter 2

1. Kramer Mills, C., & Battisto, J. (2020). *Double Jeopardy: COVID-19's Concentrated Health and Wealth Effects in Black Communities.* New York Federal Reserve, p. 1. Retrieved February 16, 2023, from https://www.newyorkfed.org/medialibrary/media/smallbusiness/DoubleJeopardy_COVID19andBlackOwnedBusinesses

2. *Racial Disparities in Paycheck Protection Program Lending.* (n.d.). NBER, p. 1. https://www.nber.org/digest/202112/racial-disparities-paycheck-protection-program-lending

3. *The New York Times.* (1968, April 26). Nixon Urges "Black Ownership" to Help Solve Racial Problems. https://www.nytimes.com/1968/04/26/archives/nixon-urges-black-ownership-to-help-solve-racial-problems.html

4. Ibid.

5. Baradaran, M. (2019). *The Color of Money: Black Banks and the Racial Wealth Gap* (Reprint). Belknap Press, an Imprint of Harvard University Press.

6. hooks, b. (2018). *All about Love: New Visions.* William Morrow Paperbacks, p. 39.

7. Ibid., p. 37.

8. Joseph, A. (2020). Why I Gave To The Runway Project—RUNWAY. RUNWAY. https://www.runway.family/blog/blog-post-title-one-zj3n2

Chapter 3

1. King, R. (2018). *Mindful of Race: Transforming Racism from the Inside Out.* Sounds True.

2. Ibid., p. 12.

3. Villanueva, E., & Barber, W. B. J., II. (2021). *Decolonizing Wealth, Second Edition: Indigenous Wisdom to Heal Divides and Restore Balance.* Berrett-Koehler Publishers.

4. *Kimberlé Crenshaw on Intersectionality, More Than Two Decades Later.* (2017, June 8). Columbia Law School. https://www.law.columbia.edu/news/archive/kimberle-crenshaw-intersectionality-more-two-decades-later

5. Krznaric, R. (2021). *The Good Ancestor: A Radical Prescription for Long-Term Thinking.* The Experiment.
6. *About.* (n.d.). The Good Ancestor Movement. Retrieved January 14, 2023, from https://www.goodancestormovement.com/about

Chapter 4

1. *Investors.* (2019, September 12). RUNWAY. https://www.runway.family/investors
2. *Lives vs. the Economy* (K. Malone & S. Gonzalez, interviewers). (2020, April 15). NPR: Planet Money. https://www.npr.org/transcripts/835571843
3. Ibid.

Chapter 5

1. *Monument of a Crime.* (n.d.). White House Historical Association (en-US). Retrieved December 4, 2022, from https://www.whitehousehistory.org/monument-of-a-crime
2. Edwards, J. H. (2022, October 27). The Freedman's Bank Forum Obscures the Bank's Real History. *Washington Post.* https://www.washingtonpost.com/made-by-history/2022/10/27/freedmans-bank-black-communities-banking/
3. *Freedman's Bank Demise.* (2023, January 23). US Department of the Treasury. https://home.treasury.gov/about/history/freedmans-bank-building/freedmans-bank-demise
4. *FDIC National Survey of Unbanked and Underbanked Households.* (2022). Federal Deposit Insurance Corporation. https://www.fdic.gov/analysis/household-survey/2021report.pdf
5. White House Historical Association, *Monument of a Crime.*
6. Du Bois, W. E. B. (2020). *The Souls of Black Folk by W.E.B. Du Bois.* Independently published, p. 10.
7. Klein, A. (2020, July 10). *Reducing Bias in AI-Based Financial Services.* Brookings Institution. https://www.brookings.edu/research/reducing-bias-in-ai-based-financial-services/
8. Homepage. (2022, August 15). Seed Commons. https://seedcommons.org
9. Du Bois, W. E. B. (2020). *The Souls of Black Folk by W. E. B. Du Bois.* Independently published.
10. Ibid.

Chapter 6

1. Archer, D. N. (2020). "White Men's Roads through Black Men's Homes": Advancing Racial Equity through Highway Reconstruction, p. 1265. Social Science Research Network. https://papers.ssrn.com/sol3/Delivery.cfm/SSRN_ID3715149_code521615.pdf?abstractid=3539889&mirid=1
2. Somé, M. P. (1997). *Ritual: Power, Healing and Community (Compass)* (1st ed.). Penguin Books, p. 73.
3. Davis, F. E. (2019). *The Little Book of Race and Restorative Justice: Black Lives, Healing, and US Social Transformation (Justice and Peacebuilding).* Good Books.
4. *Finance.* (n.d.). Ujima. Retrieved December 22, 2022, from https://www.ujimaboston.com/finance
5. Diouf, S. A. (2007). *Dreams of Africa in Alabama: The Slave Ship Clotilda and the Story of the Last Africans Brought to America.* Oxford University Press, p. 2.

6. Lee, T. (2021, November 9). How America's Vast Racial Wealth Gap Grew: By Plunder. *The New York Times*. https://www.nytimes.com/interactive/2019/08/14/magazine/racial -wealth-gap.html

7. Ibid.

8. *Restorative Economies Fund*. (2022, November 29). Kataly Foundation. https://www .katalyfoundation.org/program/restorative-economies-fund/

Chapter 7

1. Debt Stress Tears at Your Body, Too. (2008). In *Associated Press-AOL Health Poll*. Associated Press. Retrieved January 21, 2023, from http://surveys.associatedpress.com

2. Assari, S. (2019). Race, Depression, and Financial Distress in a Nationally Representative Sample of American Adults. *Brain Sciences*, *9*(2), 29. https://www.ncbi.nlm.nih.gov/pmc /articles/PMC6406793/pdf/brainsci-09-00029.pdf

3. Ibid.

4. Hasler, A., A. Lusardi, and O. Valdes. (2021). Financial Anxiety and Stress among U.S. Households: New Evidence from the National Financial Capability Study and Focus Groups, page 13. Global Financial Literacy Excellence Center. The George Washington School of Business. https://gflec.org/wp-content/uploads/2021/04/Anxiety-and-Stress -Report-GFLEC-FINRA-FINAL.pdf?x85507=

5. Kiel, P. (2014, September 15). *Unseen Toll: Wages of Millions Seized to Pay Past Debts*. Pro-Publica. https://www.propublica.org/article/unseen-toll-wages-of-millions-seized-to-pay -past-debts

6. Kiel, P. and A. Waldman. (2015, October 8). *The Color of Debt: How Collection Suits Squeeze Black Neighborhoods*. ProPublica. https://www.propublica.org/article/debt-collection-lawsuits -squeeze-black-neighborhoods

7. *1863 Fund*. (n.d.). 1863 Ventures. Retrieved December 22, 2022, from https://www .1863.fund

8. Ibid.

Chapter 8

1. King, M. L. (1966, October). *Nonviolence: The Only Road to Freedom*. Teaching American History. https://teachingamericanhistory.org/document/nonviolence-the-only-road-to -freedom

2. Smith, V. (2021). *A Narrative of the Life and Adventures of Venture, a Native of Africa, but Resident above Sixty Years in the United States of America, Related by Himself*. Aeterna.

3. Ibid., p. 24.

4. Ibid., p. 31.

5. Nembhard, J. G. (2014). *Collective Courage: A History of African American Cooperative Economic Thought and Practice* (1st ed.). Pennsylvania State University Press.

6. Ibid., p. 31.

7. Ibid., p. 32.

8. Ibid.

9. *W. E. B. Du Bois (William Edward Burghardt), 1868–1963, Ed. Economic Co-operation among Negro Americans. Report of a Study Made by Atlanta University, under the Patronage*

of the Carnegie Institution of Washington, D.C., Together with the Proceedings of the 12th Conference for the Study of the Negro Problems, Held at Atlanta University, on Tuesday, May the 28th, 1907. (n.d.). Documenting the American South. https://docsouth.unc.edu/church/dubois07/dubois.html

10. Rochester, S. D. (2018). *The Black Tax: The Cost of Being Black in America.* Good Steward Publishing.

11. *About.* (n.d.). Dr. Richard Harris House. Retrieved January 4, 2023, from https://richardharrishouse.com/about/

12. Moore, J. (2021, October 6). *First Black Female Owned Bar Will Open in Downtown Mobile Despite Racial Controversy.* NBC News, Channel 15. Retrieved February 6, 2023, from https://mynbc15.com/news/local/first-black-female-owned-bar-will-open-in-downtown-mobile-despite-racial-controversy

Chapter 9

1. Holloway, K. (2021, December 8). How Thousands of Black Farmers Were Forced Off Their Land. *The Nation.* https://www.thenation.com/article/society/black-farmers-pigford-debt/

2. Douglas, L. (2022, May 2). *U.S. Black Farmers Lost $326 Bln Worth of Land in 20th Century-Study.* Reuters. https://www.reuters.com/world/us/us-black-farmers-lost-326-bln-worth-land-20th-century-study-2022-05-02/

3. Ibid.

4. *About Us.* (2021, February 1). Slow Money Institute. https://slowmoney.org/about

5. Ibid.

6. Fullerton, J. (2015). *Regenerative Capitalism: How Universal Principles and Patterns Will Shape Our New Economy.* Capital Institute.

7. Marquis, C. (2021, September 7). RSF Is Leading the Way in Moving from Impact Investing to Regenerative Finance. *Forbes.* https://www.forbes.com/sites/christophermarquis/2021/09/07/rsf-is-leading-the-way-in-moving-from-impact-investing-to-regenerative-finance/?sh=ed75f5914f5d

Chapter 10

1. Nikole Hannah-Jones is the Pulitzer-winning journalist of the *New York Times,* 1619 Project.

2. Dubb, S. (2016, July). Interview of Elandria Williams: Highlander Center and Co-editor of Beautiful Solutions. *Community Wealth.* The interview is no longer available, though more information about Elandria can be found at http://community-wealth.org

3. "We Are Worthy" was written and published by Elandria Williams on her personal Facebook page on April 15, 2020. She passed away on September 23, 2020. Following her death, the poem has been used all over the world as a tribute to Elandria's life and legacy. The poem is reprinted courtesy of Elnora Williams.

Acknowledgments

As this book suggests, everyone needs someone to believe in them. I have been fortunate and deeply humbled by how many people have shown up to help me throughout the process of bringing the book to print. These folks are my Believe-in-You Money investors, people who poured into me to make my vision for this book possible. From my coaches to the wisdom keepers, there has been a community behind me from the very beginning.

When I had nothing but an idea, Heather believed in me. Thank you, Heather Box of Million Person Project, for helping me craft my story. As my writing coach, Heather helped me feel confident that I had good ideas and that they should be shared.

Thank you, Rha Goddess of Move The Crowd, my soul coach. The emergency check-in session with Rha got me through a tough space, when I was unsure and feeling stuck. Rha helped me see the fullness of what was possible for me and this book in the midst of challenges.

Marjorie Kelly has been one of my greatest teachers. When I called her and asked for help with this book, she did not hesitate to bring all her brilliance to *Believe-in-You Money*. Marjorie, thank you. Your early endorsement of my book was important to me, both personally and professionally, because it helped me land a beautiful partnership with Berrett-Koehler and my editor, Steve Piersanti.

The day I submitted my book proposal to Steve, I was a nervous wreck. The next day, after reading his email response, I felt a returned sense of ease and peace. In his email, he told me that he remembered hearing my name before—actually it was years before—and he didn't want to pass on the chance to work with me again. I was honored. Steve's commitment to and excitement about publishing books that change the world became the glue that bonded us. I am here because Steve believed in me. Thank you so much, Steve. To the entire Berrett-Koehler community—from the design team to the sales team to all the other authors who gave me advice—thank you for your support and warm welcome.

Writing about race, business, finance, repair, and healing is not easy. To be most effective, it requires striking a balance among history, data, and humanity in a way that inspires us to action. I was constantly asking myself, How do I make this readable and relatable? How do I say the hard things and still leave room for hope? Questions like these tugged at me during this process. Thankfully, I did not have to hold these questions alone. dana fitchett was there every step of the way, helping me find the right tone and right language by bringing a critical equity lens to the editing process. I owe so much to her for the deep amounts of love, friendship, patience, and organization that she put into this work; it made all the difference.

Thank you to the powerful communications team surrounding this book, which is led by my dear friend Amy Hartzler of Do Good Better Communications, along with Guinevere Higgins and graphic designer Tigi Kelkay. A special thank-you to the production team who created the supplemental video communications for the project, led by producer Kareece Lawrence and director Garreth Daley of GD Films. And thank you to my podcast family at *Road to Repair*, Nikishka Iyengar and Andrew X, for helping me share more about this book.

Believe-in-You Money features several interviews and endorsements from people whom I call the wisdom keepers: people I trust and admire in this work for equity and justice. In Afro-Indigenous customs, wisdom keepers bring forward our ancient traditions through their stories and their techniques in order to move us toward a more conscious, peaceful, and sustainable world.

I am forever grateful to the wisdom and words of

- Nwamaka Agbo, Kataly Foundation
- adrienne maree brown, author of *Emergent Strategy*
- LaTosha Brown, Black Voters Matter
- Tarana Burke, me too. Movement
- Anu Gupta, Be More with Anu
- Dr. Henry Louis Gates, Harvard University
- Konda Mason, Jubilee Justice
- Sonya Renee Taylor, author of *The Body Is Not an Apology*
- Pastor Andrew Wilkes, The Double Love Experience
- *Elandria Williams, in tribute*

And to all the family and friends who took care of my heart through this journey, I thank you. In particular I thank Lynne Hoey and Dr. Janelle Williams for the great conversations that brought that fun mix of critical thinking and big laughs.

Thank you, Rani Langer-Croager. I don't know what I would do without you. You have been the force behind so much that we have accomplished. I am grateful for our sisterhood and our shared belief in the power of the people.

Thank you to my fellowship families: Harvard University, Stanford University, Southern University, Duke University, University of South Alabama, Just Economy Institute, Nathan Cummings Foundation, Common Future, and Center for Economic Democracy.

Thank you to my Boston family: Malia Lazu, Professors Marcyliena Morgan and Larry Bobo, and Sherina McKinley.

Thank you to my Chicago family: all my cousins on the South Side, especially Jenigh Garrett, as well as my college friends—in particular,

Tamika Lee-Robinson and family, and my friend and sorority sister, by way of Detroit, Cortney Hicks-Lanier.

Thank you to my Mobile family: all my cousins in Prichard, my bestie Chandra Brown-Stewart, my brothers and mom Stephani. A special thank-you to my dad, former mayor Jesse Norwood, for being with me every step of the way. I have never had a more faithful friend than you.

Thank you to my Kingston family: Takema Robinson-Llewellyn and family, Natalie Reid and Andrew Bailey for taking care of my heart, mind, body, and spirit. Whether going to the beach, music concerts, or yoga class, getting massages, or just spending time with one another, I'm grateful for it all.

Thank you to the RUNWAY family: Alicia, Nina, Lauren, Tomme, Naima, Laurika, Jaimie, Konda, and especially Jamica, for your tireless work to help me realize a world where the economy loves Black people. You are the definition of cool people. Thank you to all the people who have invested in RUNWAY's work, with a huge hug to my good friends Kate and Tiffany at Chordata Capital, and a deep thank-you to each company that allows us to finance your dreams. The faith you have in us is why we are able to do what we do.

I am the living proof of my ancestors' hard work, imagination, and *faith*. I thank God for the opportunity to stand in their legacies and share my ideas as I call for our collective activation of faith in something better. I feel deep gratitude for the bounty of blessings that this book has provided and will provide. May the words in this book inspire hundreds more books that will lead us to peace.

And to my mama, my forever angel: Marvelle J. Manga-Mixon, the power of your spirit is the wind beneath my wings; together we will go to all the places and see all the things.

Index

About the Author

Jessica Norwood is an entrepreneur, investor, artist, and philanthropist who has spent her career exploring the ways that money can be an expression of repair and spiritual care. She is a serial social entrepreneur who works with a community of investors to provide Believe-in-You Money as a way to create an economy that loves Black people and encourages others to do the same.

As the founder and CEO of RUNWAY, Jessica leads alongside a powerhouse team of women of color who are committed to resourcing Black founders by providing start-up capital and nurturing their ongoing success. Each leader at RUNWAY brings a unique skill set to the organization's shared purpose: to advance resilience for Black businesses and the communities they serve, through practices and infrastructure that close the racial wealth gap for good.

Widely recognized for her financial activism, Jessica is a former fellow of the Center for Economic Democracy and RSF Social Finance's Integrated Capital Institute (now called Just Economy Institute), winner of the prestigious Nathan Cummings Foundation Fellowship, a former BALLE (now called Common Future) Local Economy Fellow, and the Political Power and Social Change fellow of the Hip Hop Archive at the Hutchins Center of Harvard University, as well as a lifelong fellow of the Sanford School of Public Policy at Duke University and Southern University College of Business for Emerging Leaders. Her participation and leadership in these programs have deeply informed groundbreaking work on restorative and reparative economies and Black entrepreneurship.

Jessica's innovative work has been profiled on National Public Radio and Bloomberg Television and in *Essence Magazine, Next City, Fast Company*, and *Conscious Company*. Edgar Villanueva, author of *New York Times* best-seller *Decolonizing Wealth*, considers her work the "medicine" modern philanthropy and investment need. She is the cohost of the podcast *Road to Repair*; has spoken at events for communities of change makers including Net Impact, Social Capital Markets, Community Capital, Slow Money, Social Venture Institute, and Social Venture Circle; and has served on boards including the Highlander Research and Education Center and Emergent Strategies Institute.

Jessica was raised in Alabama, where she continues to support local work. Her career and approach to reparative economics have been deeply informed by her roots in Chicago, Oakland, and Boston. She currently lives in both Alabama and Kingston, Jamaica, where she continues to deepen her commitment to and investment in Black joy and liberation across the diaspora. Having lived all over the world, Jessica has found that her heart sings most when at the beach, next to deep and far-reaching waters.

Anyone who knows Jessica knows she is an artist, and she is her own palette, with a love of fashion, jewelry, art, and all things creative. She is a natural weaver, moving across communities of financial activists, futurists, wisdom keepers, and culture shapers with grace, beauty, and humor. Jessica is a natural host and loves to gather people for food, conversation, and good trouble.

About RUNWAY

RUNWAY is a financial innovation firm that is wholeheartedly committed to dismantling systemic barriers and creatively reimagining the financial policies and practices that hold these barriers in place—all in the name of Black liberation.

RUNWAY works with financial institutions to develop funds and create practices rooted in love. While it may seem ironic to reference love and financial institutions in the same sentence, the pairing of the two is not only possible but actively being leveraged in the interest of a healed economy. RUNWAY is a community of practice for financial institutions that desire to show up differently and provides a community of support for entrepreneurs. Bringing together methodologies of character-based underwriting, untraditional assessment of capital readiness, and community-led lending, RUNWAY signals the love of friends and family.

The true crux of RUNWAY is an invitation for entrepreneurs to feel the love and confidence that is possible when they get the financial support that they need, and an invitation for investors and philanthropists to approach capital in a far less extractive and more regenerative way. RUNWAY invites financial institutions to authentically connect to Black-owned businesses and invites local communities to utilize RUNWAY's infrastructure and methodologies to develop community-based funds that mirror the realities of their own investment needs and desires.

RUNWAY began in the aftermath of Hurricane Katrina, which exposed the racial wealth gap between Black and White households. Reports at the time reflected a gap of over $100,000. The lack of access to economic securities, aid, resources, and care, along with the absence of capital for Black businesses, hindered the recovery and resilience of the affected communities. RUNWAY, founded by Jessica Norwood and led by a team of Black and Brown women, saw a need for equity-centered solutions and set out to create them.

Since then, RUNWAY has been developing and cocreating funds, helping financial institutions shift policies, and building the infrastructure that reflects the equitable world Black entrepreneurs need. At the onset of the pandemic, RUNWAY met with its community of entrepreneurs to ask what support they needed during this unprecedented time of uncertainty. The answer? A financial headrest. RUNWAY launched a six-month pilot of universal basic income and loan deferment. The organization's actions resulted in a 100 percent survival rate for its businesses, a testament to its dedication to providing transformational, trust-based solutions that work.

For RUNWAY, the future relies on collective action and community leadership that allows the next generations to bring to life the thriving Black businesses they know we need. This more liberated and equitable future relies on the creativity and detail of an artist approaching a blank canvas with an aim to root into the transformational splendor of the Black imagination while igniting collective resistance strategies. Learn more at runway.family.

Dear reader,

Thank you for picking up this book and welcome to the worldwide BK community! You're joining a special group of people who have come together to create positive change in their lives, organizations, and communities.

What's BK all about?

Our mission is to connect people and ideas to create a world that works for all.

Why? Our communities, organizations, and lives get bogged down by old paradigms of self-interest, exclusion, hierarchy, and privilege. But we believe that can change. That's why we seek the leading experts on these challenges—and share their actionable ideas with you.

A welcome gift

To help you get started, we'd like to offer you a **free copy** of one of our bestselling ebooks:

www.bkconnection.com/welcome

When you claim your **free ebook**, you'll also be subscribed to our blog.

Our freshest insights

Access the best new tools and ideas for leaders at all levels on our blog at ideas.bkconnection.com.

Sincerely,

Your friends at Berrett-Koehler

MIX
Paper from
responsible sources
FSC® C016245

Certified
Corporation